DIRECT PARTICIPATION IN ACTION: THE NEW BUREAUCRACY

The views expressed in this book are personal to the authors and do not represent statements of official policy

Direct participation in action: the new bureaucracy

DAVID PACE and
JOHN HUNTER

SAXON  HOUSE

British Library Cataloguing in Publication Data

Pace, David E
  Direct participation in action.
  1. Employees' representation in management –
  Great Britain 2. Electronic data processing
  personnel – Great Britain
  I. Title II. Hunter, John
  354'.41'00172   HD5660.G7

  ISBN 0-566-00205-1

Published by Saxon House in association with Gower Press
Teakfield Limited, Westmead, Farnborough, Hants., England.

ISBN 0 566 00205 1

Manufactured in England by Short Run Publishing Services.

Printed and bound by Ilfadrove Limited, Barry, Glamorgan
S. Wales

Contents

Foreword

My first reaction on reading this book, of which my view can in no way be detached, was to feel that an alternative title might be "And the lion shall lie down with the lamb". For the initiative of the Civil Service Department's Job Satisfaction Team, with which we in general very fully co-operated, has as I see it led to the questioning of many of the stances adopted by each one of us in our various working relationships. Whether it is management and staff, official side and unions, Census and Stats, programmers and operators, whatever the potential conflict, the attempt has been and is being made to see the differences for what they are and generally the extent of the common ground has been enough to overcome them.

During the years we have been exposed in the Civil Service to propaganda for many forms of management, but the concepts which are the foundations of this book, though unfortunately in practice they have been given the name of "Participative Management", are totally different in nature, and not just in degree, from those underlying any of the other so-called systems of management.

As I understand it the basic concept is that every adult is only properly fulfilled if he is able to express his potentialities freely, unfettered by others but sensibly controlled by himself in accordance with the needs of his fellows. Our civilisation in all its facets has developed in ways which have deliberately or inadvertently limited this freedom, and such limitations appear to have had a tendency to persist and even increase unnecessarily. Society now attempts in many ways to dispense with these limitations. The work of the Job Satisfaction Team, though not expressed in these terms, is one such attempt. The significance for individuals and groups, whether they be management, unions or working sections are manifold. If a person or group is freed from a particular constriction he will grow in a new way and such growth can be painful as well as intensely rewarding. In Computer Division we have experienced these different facets and the growth continues and will hopefully spread.

P. H. KENNEY
HEAD OF COMPUTER DIVISION

Preface

In many areas of society at the present time there is a widespread and growing interest in the concepts of participation and industrial democracy. Many people have come to accept these ideas as desirable changes that need to be made in our forms of work organisation. However, the practical implications of such changes and the demands they make on individuals and groups are not widely recognised and are difficult to understand.

This book is a description of a consultancy project undertaken in a public sector ADP organisation. The main theme of the project was the development of direct participation within the organisation; this book is an attempt to describe the events and processes of the project, the social context in which it took place, and the outcomes of the work as far as they can be assessed so far. The book also attempts to identify and clarify the important issues that emerged during the development of these participative processes.

After two years of working closely with management, staff and unions we feel able to draw some broad conclusions about participation at work. We try to indicate some lessons and guidelines for future organisational policy and we conclude that "The New Bureaucracy" is both viable and necessary if a future crisis in our large public and private bureaucracies is to be averted.

These ideas have developed from our experience of the broad programme of work undertaken in the Civil Service by its Job Satisfaction Team. Thus the approach we argue in this book has a broader basis than the one project described in detail here. We would therefore particularly like to acknowledge the contribution made to our thinking by all the past and present members of the Job Satisfaction Team, civil servants and consultants, as well as many of the civil servants and union officers we met during our work with the Team. A broader treatment of the work of the Team is being prepared by Keith Robertson and will be published shortly.

1 The Social Context of Participation

An important element in the understanding of the project that will be described in the main body of the work is the social context in which it took place. Indeed, the project itself could be looked on as social experimentation within a working community - the experiment reflecting the changes we perceive in society at large. It is therefore sensible to begin with a review of the changes that are taking place in society and the impact of these changes on people at work.

Few would doubt that western society is undergoing rapid change, but any attempt to analyse what is in fact occuring is to some extent impressionistic and must necessarily be couched in tentative terms - for in effect one is attempting to write history as it happens! Whether or not the analysis is right, it is important because it is how we, the consultants setting up the project, interpret social trends.

The Post War trends towards Planning and Control

A significant feature of social structure today is its corporate nature and the domination of society by large powerful coalitions of interest. J K Galbraith [1] has given an excellent description of the pressures upon industrial organisations to seek to control their environment and create a degree of certainty for their operations. Since the market situation is uncertain the aim of the giant corporations has been to replace the market with a planned environment. Thus the corporations have sought to extend control over supply and demand. On the supply side control has been extended largely by vertical and horizontal integration. The merger movement of the 1960's was an important manifestation of this. Supply of capital has been secured by giant organisations largely generating their own cash. On the demand side control operates by such means as built in obsolescence and aggressive advertising. The replacement of competition with collusion, Galbraith argues, is mainly because of the necessity, given today's technological complexity, to commit vast sums to development expenditure and investment prior to sales. So large and powerful have some organisations become they can in fact pose a threat to the national sovereignty of smaller industrial countries.

Concurrent with the growth of multinational and national corporations in the private sector has been the growth in size of government and trade union organisations. Though in part a defensive response to the development of huge private sector corporations, the main thrust towards increased size in public sector and union organisations has again come from pressures arising from scale and complexity. Planning and centralised control appear to be the logical answer to these pressures. Attitudes towards the extent to which governments should intervene in the economic and social life of a nation have changed markedly,

1

particularly since the Second World War. Keynsian economics and the post war commitment to full employment ushered in a new area of government activity. Before the war the resolution of the first order economic problems of full employment and the deployment of the basic economic resources, (land, labour and capital), had, in general, been left to impersonal market forces. With the growth of economic demand management in the 1950's and 60's and the initiatives towards a more planned economy, governments found themselves more and more involved in the minutiae of economic life. Increasingly large bureaucratic organisations became necessary to support this more interventionist role.

Governments have also accepted, and have been expected to accept, greater responsibilities in the social field. In Britain, there have been particular influences such as the demand for greater security (economic and social), the opportunities for longer, more liberal education, much greater geographical and social mobility, the influx of different ethnic minority groups and an ageing population. A developing social consciousness has been manifested in successive piecemeal attempts to deal with these problems. The resulting patchwork of legislation has created an organisational and procedural maze of dismaying size and complexity.

Political developments have also given impetus to the creation of more bureaucracy. The establishment of the EEC appeared almost inevitable if Europe was to retain any influence in a world of polarised power blocs. The potential scale of the bureaucracy here is breathtaking. Apart from major issues such as establishing common agricultural policies, harmonising tax systems, and developing social policies on a multi national scale, even the pint of beer must become transformed into either a half or a whole litre and the humble sausage to be eaten by hundreds of millions of people must apparently be standardised.

The way business is organised and transacted - the technology of work - has also added momentum to the trend for increased organisational size and bureaucractic inflation in the public sector. Here, perhaps more than in the private sector, values which lay great stress on the benefits to be derived from centralisation, specialisation and standardisation, have had great influence on organisational structure and design. Though it is difficult to argue against the application of these concepts at earlier stages of industrial development it seems likely that their continued uncritical adoption, particularly during such periods of rapid technological change as the post war years, has been counter-productive. It seems that the nature of government work, with its need for uniformity and equity, coupled with the scale of operations, has meant that the apparent logic for the adoption of extensive, routinised systems has rarely been brought into question. Specialisation and fragmentation of work have been raised to the status of a virtue because they were thought to lead to increased efficiency, and the advent of the computer has encouraged and made possible some of the worst excesses in this field.

The end result of the continued pursuit of this philosophy of organisational design has been the large, complex and centralised government machine that is so familiar to us in the mid 70s.

Pressures to Bureaucratise

Examine the size of organisations in the public sector and their rate of growth. The nationalised industries are the largest, but these apart, there were 565,000 non-industrial civil servants in 1975 compared to 315,000 in 1965, a manpower increase of 80%. The influence of the public sector organisations is immense as they control nearly 60% of total national spending. In 1976/77 the social security programme alone accounted for £9578 million (Department of Health and Social Security 80,000+ employees) defence, £5835, (Ministry of Defence, 200,000+ employees) and the rate support for local government £7522 (Department of the Environment 80,000+ employees).

The final authority legitimising the activity of these Government departments is the legislature. In a democratic country this implies that any activity carried out by the executive Civil Service is open to public scrutiny and comparison against the law. The principle of equality before the law produces pressures for uniformity and consistency in administering the law. Not only must activity rigidly comply with the letter of the law but administration must also be seen to be prudently and economically performed. It is these pressures for public accountability (some say pressures which are unreasonably demanding), together with the scale and nature of the task which largely determine the form of organisation in the Civil Service. The scale is vast. For instance Income Tax is collected from over 20 million workers and unemployment benefit is at the time of writing paid to 1.5 million recipients. Value Added Tax is collected from over 1 million traders all of whom are periodically visited. Not only is the scale vast but the complexity has increased and changes have become more frequent. Consider an example of the calculation of a quarterly assessment of VAT from a small trader:

$$\text{Taking } £19,183.65 \times \frac{4407.14}{19806.31} \times \frac{2}{27} \times \frac{1}{8} = £335.72$$

After deducting his input tax the net payment to the revenue would probably be about £40; but not even the pence may be decreased.

In 1974 alone the VAT rate on petrol changed from 0% to 10% to 8% to 25%.

Another example can be drawn from welfare provisions. A report produced by the Supplementary Benefits Commission 1976, chaired by Professor Donnison, suggested that Supplementary Benefit procedures had become so complicated that even the officials who administered the scheme could not understand them. Four and a half million people, (1 in 11 of the population), received £1300 million a year in benefit. Attempts to try to give relief according

3

to particular individual needs have increased the complexity of the regulations to such an extent that the number of staff administering Supplementary Benefit has risen from 12,000 in 1966 to 30,000 in 1976.

In order to cope with those pressures of public accountability, scale, complexity and change, public sector organisations act in a seemingly rational manner. The jargon of the statute book is interpreted centrally and broken down into rules and procedures which are embodied in codes of instructions for staff to follow. Most action is conducted by way of the written word, and extensive records are maintained. Even with such detailed instructions, different interpretations can be applied so that precedents are recorded to ensure absolute consistency. The scale and complexity is dealt with in the traditional way by breaking down the task into categories of work and employing strict division of labour. The organisations are hierarchically structured with each level having a rigidly prescribed task and responsibilities within its particular area of specialisation.

The pressures in the public service have thus produced a technical system which is almost a pure form of Weberian bureaucracy. On balance it has served well in the past, and has produced a civil service reckoned to be among the finest in the world. Our concern is that an uncritical reliance on the methods which brought success in the past may bring about a crisis in the future.

Society as a Bureaucracy

A series of TV programmes shown in 1976 sought to investigate "Why is Britain becoming harder to Govern?" The question posed was why was it that way back in the 1960s almost everyone took Britain's political institutions for granted and accepted she would remain in the future what she had been in the past, a tolerant liberal democracy, whereas in the mid 70s this was no longer certain. The commentators agreed that some of the developments such as the decline in support for established political parties and the disappearance of a moral and religious concensus could be observed equally well abroad. The British thinkers agreed however that the fault lay somewhere in the system - in the relationship of individuals to the means of production and to one another. We believe that a major part of the explanation for behaviour indicating dissent and disillusionment with aspects of life in society today lies in the workplace, in the way it is organised and in the way people are managed there.

We have argued that change, particularly the increases in scale and complexity in the economic, social, political and technological spheres, has led to much more highly developed planning and control. This is a seemingly rational response but these developments have tended to ignore the human dimension in organisational life. Scale and centralisation have increased to the point where society itself may be seen as a large bureaucratic organisation. These giant organisations in society at large - the corporate state - invade peoples lives at many points and largely determine the quality and style of life for huge

4

populations. The bureaucratic nature of the structure is reflected in the nature of the policies that emanate from the structure. Where such policies derive from authority delegated by statute to a government department the bureaucratic nature of action, (literally - 'rule by officials'), is heightened. The increasingly common delegation of authority by Parliament to government departments which are not subject to the full democratic monitoring of such authority is again a symptom of increasing scale and complexity.

It is certainly possible to see a reaction in society against size and centralisation, the impersonalisation of much of life today and the loss of a sense of identification. Challenging bureaucratic influences is an attempt by people to re-assert a degree of control over their own lives. Reactions and diverse initiatives which might be cited as examples of such challenges are - community action programmes, the devolution movement in Scotland and Wales, the 3rd London Airport pressure group, the Campaign for Real Ale, and the development of the worker participation movement. These can all be seen in various ways as reactions against the impersonal and remote forces of authority which fail to take account of individual interests, or local aspirations. These, largely self help, movements have succeeded in persuading the impersonal forces to concede that democratic rights of individuals and minority groups do exist. The significant fact is they have had some success.

The employee's perspective of bureaucracy

There are signs then that society at large is able to mobilise forces to modify bureaucratic policies to some extent; the question we must examine is whether or not bureaucratic organisations will be able to adapt when these same forces are brought within their boundaries. The citizens attitudes and values do not dramatically change when he puts on his employee hat. For if no adaption by employing organisations takes place the effect of these forces will be negative and could be manifested in greater degrees of apathy, lethargy, resignation, bloody mindedness, sullenness and lack of interest. These are well documented psychological reactions to frustration and there is no doubt managers are becoming increasingly worried about the growth of these attitudes and the consequences which can threaten a firm's very existence. Sit ins, strikes, bad work, absenteeism, poor time keeping are all symptoms of this underlying malaise.

The general public's reaction to the trend towards bureacracy in society at large (the customer attitude) bears sharply upon the individual employee in the public sector, particularly those involved in face to face relationships with the general public. Apart from this reflection of the wider social climate within which he works the employee in a bureaucracy experiences a working environment and climate which is, far too often, out of tune with his expectations and self image.

5

The employee working in a bureaucracy experiences a hierarchial structure with authority legitimised by established rules, and sanctions, the most important of which is the withholding of promotion and career advancement. Responsibility for decision making is laid down for each level in the hierarchy. Relationships between functional areas and hierarchial levels tend to be formal, task structures are rigidly and often narrowly defined, and individual discretion is strictly circumscribed.

W E Moore [2] has suggested that bureaucracies have the virtue of securing co-operation between large numbers of persons without those people necessarily feeling co-operative. This view may well have been true in the past but a widening of the gap between the values of the individual and those of the organisation may generate unco-operative behaviour. People today, and particularly young people are encouraged to be more critical of ideas and authority than their predecessors. Personal relationships are less formal. Managers are no longer always accorded automatic deference and courtesy nor can they rely on an unquestioning attitude by staff who may believe certain work practices and procedures to be unintelligent or inappropriate. Sofer [3] wrote "it appears to be a distinct component of contemporary man that he is in a state of tension that is discharged in action to master his physical and human environments, to demonstrate and test his capacities and to express his definitions of the desirable". Bureaucratic man cannot discharge this state of tension if his actions are rigidly prescribed, he cannot therefore master his work environment in any true sense or test his capacities. He remains an instrument of production. He cannot express his definitions of the desirable for there is, in general, no effective mechanism to allow this to take place.

The Crucial Problem

In short we see as the crucial problem that people in society at large, and in organisations in particular, are rejecting the traditional rules of obedience - be it respect for the authority of the parent, school, church or employer. They are restless, seeking new relationships, which incorporate more freedom, and are confused about what form the relationships might take. The devolution and industrial democracy movements clearly display the characteristics of the confusion. No one has been this way before. In work organisations we are facing the prospect of an emancipated work face for the first time in history. There is likely to be much institutional inertia preventing the manumission of the mass of employees. What are needed are relationships which allow a balance combining sufficient freedom for people with the discipline necessary for the effective operation of any cooperative interprise. We offer here a description of a practical exploration of the problem and of an attempt to create a climate which would enable employees at all levels the opportunity to exercise a greater influence on their work environment. Specifically we try to answer four questions:

Is it possible to establish such a climate?

How do you go about doing it?

Does it work?

Does it last?

NOTES

[1]   Galbraith, J.K. The New Industrial State, Hamish Hamilton, 1967.

[2]   Moore, W.E. The Conduct of the Corporation, Random House 1962

[3]   Sofer, C. Organisations in Theory and Practice, Heinemann, 1972

2 An Introduction to Computer Division

The last 20 years have seen an enormous growth in the use of computers in the public service. By the beginning of 1976 there were some 120 computer installations serving the Civil Service at a capital cost of £70 million and with approaching 17,000 people directly employed in them about - £140-worth of computer power per civil servant. This big commitment, in terms of capital and labour (generally high qualified labour), is matched by the widespread influence that computers now have in a large number of key operational areas in the public sector. Whole blocks of work - payroll, stores and accounting, the payment of social security benefits, the collection and interpretation of statistics (employment, trade, education, business and population) - are now completely dependent on the computer and the smooth day-to-day running of the business of government itself increasingly relies on computers and their associated technology.

Increasing reliance and dependence on one particular technology, and particularly on a technology which concentrates so intensely the storage and processing of data and information, leads rapidly to a serious state of vulnerability. Computer systems are vulnerable not only to the technical vagaries of the hardware or inconsistency in their internal logic but also to the whims and behaviour of their human components; and it is the latter problems which prove the least predictable and tractable and which are potentially the most serious. Industrial unrest, disruption of production, even sabotage could, if widespread, be extremely damaging, even paralysing; less dramatic symptoms of disaffection such as absenteeism and low productivity can have disturbing long term implications.

The human side of computing therefore is beginning to receive more attention in the public service as some of the potentially dangerous implications of ignoring it become apparent. This was one of the main reasons why the Central Computer Agency, the central unit responsible for computing policy in the public service, commissioned some research by the Civil Service Job Satisfaction Team into the human aspects of working in ADP installations. The team, composed of both civil servants and outside consultants, was first formed in 1971 and a dozen or so major projects have subsequently been undertaken in a variety of departments. The original idea was for a series of job satisfaction studies to be mounted in different government departments to illustrate the scope for, and effects of, redesigning jobs in such a way as to increase the interest of the work and give staff more opportunity for worthwhile achievement. It was hoped that experiments of this kind would have a catalytic effect, encouraging managers throughout the Civil Service to pay more attention to the content of people's jobs. Previous work of this kind had been mainly confined to the private sector and manufacturing industry. The team was in fact led during the project described here by Keith Robertson who conducted the well known job enrichment studies in ICI [1]. From the beginning, it was recognised that the approach might well have to be adapted to meet the conditions encountered: public accountability and other features of Civil Service organisation and tradition might well inhibit the restructuring of jobs. On the other hand, job satisfaction - as the phrase implies - is not something done to people, it is something that people experience. Concern for the quality of that experience cannot be compartmentalised into a management technique; it necessitates, rather, an unaccustomed flexibility of approach. Not surprisingly, therefore, the work has evolved considerably over the last five years. All that has remained constant is the original concern for job satisfaction as such.

The authors are civil servants and were members of the Job Satisfaction Team at the time of the Central Computer Agency approach. We were assigned to the project which emerged as a request to carry out a diagnostic survey of job satisfaction in the computer division of a major government statistical office. It is worth stressing again at this point that our remit was purely one of investigation, diagnosis and research. There was no suggestion at that time of any further project activity beyond the diagnostic report stage, although we were obviously interested in that possibility. In the event the involvement of the two authors from beginning the initial diagnosis to finally leaving the organisation lasted two years.

It might be as well before launching into a description of the organisation and our activities to say a few words about the way we approached the diagnosis itself. We were trying to investigate two major areas. First, what were the features of the whole working situation that had a bearing on people's job satisfaction and their attitudes to work eg

> The people themselves (age, education and experience)
>
> The work itself (casework, repetitive, policy, craft)
>
> The technology (clerical, computer, instructions)
>
> The organisational structure (the way work was organised, functional or hierarchic, organic and informal)
>
> The degree of change
>
> The physical environment

These were all hard data; to do with facts and figures. Secondly, less tangible and probably more critical in our kind of work, how did the staff experience the complex situation created by all these influences and what attitudes and behaviour did it produce? eg

> Style of management (an expression of managerial reaction to the environment)

Organisational climate

Frustrations, difficulties, likes and dislikes

Perceptions and expectations

Needs and desires (job satisfaction being a fulfilment of personal needs and
desires)

These are all soft data; things much less easy to quantify or to be precise about.
Although we did use some survey instruments to give us a lead into important
areas, the interpretation of this soft data involved our own personal values and
judgement to a large extent.

We saw our main task as collecting the relevant hard and soft data and
matching it. For instance, it was particularly important in this study to see how
the needs and expectations of the staff matched up with the kind of
organisational environment they were working in. We then had to present the
conclusions in a way that made sense of a whole range of diverse and often
conflicting views, comments and opinions. We recognised also another important
consideration; that the diagnosis was not a once and for all thing. In the physical
sciences attempts to measure a substance may change the substance itself; thus
in a job satisfaction diagnosis the very presence of outsiders asking pointed
questions about job satisfaction and other issues may create a new situation.

Perhaps the term methodology is too exact a term for the way we gathered,
analysed and presented the data since it implies an ordered procedure, and we
sometimes felt disordered and unprofessional in our approach. However, certain
clear principles underlay what we were trying to do. One of these threads of
philosophy emerged in the way we presented the data we gathered. We saw it as
a critical part of the diagnosis that any report we produced should be a report of
the views of the staff - as someone put it "letting the staff speak for themselves".
These were the people who were experiencing the reality of their working
environment; their views must be the ones to be heard. It was our task to
provide the vehicle for those views. There were problems inherent in this
approach; for instance there were accusations that we were one-sided and that
our report was biased. Other people suggested that we were deliberately seeking
out dissatisfaction and dissatisfied people and "stirring things up". Our reaction
to this was to suggest that this kind of reporting was legitimate when the subject
of the enquiry was the views, attitudes and job satisfaction of a body of people.
We did not represent the idiosyncratic or extreme views, but attempted to
reflect the broad concensus. We did not believe that people invented things to
discuss at our interviews, but it was true that questioning made some people
think analytically about their work, possibly for the first time in some cases.
This was where diagnosis in this kind of work became more than just fact finding
or opinion gathering; it became the first phase in a broader consultancy
intervention. We were beginning to make people themselves think about and

10

question the work and how they felt about it. Another problem with this kind of approach was that an enormously diverse and sometimes conflicting range of issues emerged and it was necessary, within the general philosophy of "letting the people speak for themselves" to identify only the broad, generally agreed issues to make the task manageable.

Having set the scene as to how we came to arrive at the location, let us now consider what we found when we got there.

The office in which we found ourselves is a small government department, headed by a professional statistician, which has the responsibility for collecting and interpreting the whole range of vital statistics concerned with the population of Great Britain. It designs and directs the 10 yearly census of population, it oversees the collection of birth, death and marriage statistics and also conducts a series of important social surveys among which the General Household Survey is perhaps the most well-known. The Office includes a number of professional staff who interpret the statistics that are collected; but it will also be clear that the collection and processing of personal information on a national scale presents a massive problem for the storage, handling and analysis of data - a problem which the computer is clearly the right instrument to solve. Computer Division was set up as a direct result of an internal review of the organisation and structure of the department in 1970. This recommended that a new computer service division should be created to meet the data processing requirements of the functional divisions in the department. The new division would have wide ranging responsibilities

- the efficient operation of all the departments computers

- all data preparation

- providing a program and systems analysis service for the department

and would be managed independently of the customer divisions. A firm of commercial ADP consultants was engaged to assist with the design and establishment of the division, which had become operational a year before we carried out the diagnosis.

The creation of this new organisation was a big undertaking and would, in its own right, have represented a major step forward in the development of a more effective ADP capacity. When we also took into account the extent of the other changes in the organisation, technology and the work itself that had been experienced in the recent past the size of the achievement became apparent. It is worth cataloguing these changes;

Technology

- the introduction of complex and sophisticated new computer operating systems (George III)

11

-   the new ICL 1906S computer and the occupation of the new computer block

Work

-   the introduction of new ADP documentation standards (three volumes)

-   the changes in data streams resulting from changes in local authority boundaries and the reorganisation of the NHS

-   changing from three to two shift working

Organisation

-   the seting up of Computer Division itself

-   a rapid expansion of staff numbers

-   the introduction of several new senior managers from other departments and an additional tier of management to co-ordinate the increased scale of operations

-   very rapid promotions, particularly at the executive Officer grade level.

It was clear that management and staff had been under severe pressure to implement a wide range of changes in a very short time. That the organisation existed and was working was an impressive achievement and spoke volumes for the ability, hard work and adaptability of all concerned.

Apart from this degree of change, four other factors seem to be important in the work environment - the nature of the task being performed, the kind of people employed, the type of organisation they were working in, and the technology they used. There were naturally other factors which also helped to create the work climate, but these seemed to us the most important.

The Nature of the Task

At its simplest, the task of Computer Division was to provide an integrated and effective data processing capability for the office. This meant that the division was responsible for processing the data which flowed from central Government activity in the creation of social statistics - census, population and medical statistics and social survey findings. Although at first glance there seemed likely to be a good deal of similarity between these work requirements, in fact there were some important variations. Very crudely, census work can be envisaged as a series of very large one-off projects which may take several years

12

of planning to complete, which will rarely be repeated and which all feed from the huge data store of 58 million records which a full census creates. Statistics work, on the other hand, whilst it too has one-off projects, has a substantial repetitive element to it, not only with the processing of normal registration work (births, deaths and marriages) but also with the investigation and monitoring of other topics of particular social interest. Social survey work, whilst similar to census work in that most of its projects are not often repeated, differs markedly in that the samples chosen are, in the main, tiny by comparison and the data handling and processing problems are consequently of a different order of magnitude. Thus each area of work has its own particular flavour.

Each area also had its own traditions and history which the creation of Computer Division had not erased. We detected strong affiliations amongst staff at all levels to a particular body of work; the position of your desk in the office might be determined by whether you were "census" or "stats", and the composition of teams at social events was more likely to be determined by these same historic considerations than by present branch membership; on several occasions during the course of the diagnosis these loyalties were mentioned in the context of operational and organisational difficulties by people at quite senior levels. These former "tribal" loyalties often die hard, but can sometimes provide a valuable sense of identity for groups of staff drawn into new and large organisations. Trouble may arise when such allegiances become magnified and lead to rivalries and conflict within a new organisation.

The Organisation

The organisation of Computer Division consisted of seven branches which had responsibilities for clearly defined aspects of the work. The design was functional rather than project based and separated systems analysis, programming and production work into individual accountable branches reporting direct to the head of the Division. A further operational branch was Service Branch, designed to deal with unscheduled or ad hoc demands on the system. In addition, there were small separate branches for dealing with staff development and operating standards, and resource management. The seventh branch was Survey Branch which handled all the computing for Social Survey Division. This did not fit neatly into the structure of the organisation; it was situated in London and lived a separate, nearly autonomous, existence. Figure 1 shows how the Division was organised at that time.

The rationale behind this design was logical and simple. In theory, it channelled all contracts from customer divisions through either Planning or Service Branches, where new work was specified thoroughly before it was passed on to Programming and later Production in a natural sequence of events. This allowed the specialist groups to concentrate on their particular area of expertise without interruption or distraction.

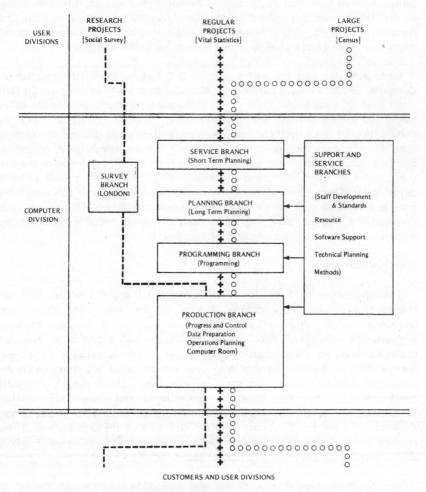

USER DIVISIONS

RESEARCH PROJECTS
[Social Survey]

REGULAR PROJECTS
[Vital Statistics]

LARGE PROJECTS
{Census}

COMPUTER DIVISION

SURVEY BRANCH (LONDON)

SERVICE BRANCH
(Short Term Planning)

PLANNING BRANCH
(Long Term Planning)

PROGRAMMING BRANCH
(Programming)

PRODUCTION BRANCH
(Progress and Control
Data Preparation
Operations Planning
Computer Room)

SUPPORT AND SERVICE BRANCHES

(Staff Development & Standards

Resource

Software Support

Technical Planning

Methods)

CUSTOMERS AND USER DIVISIONS

Figure 1.   Computer Division; as at November 1975

14

The philosophy behind the organisation was one of clear and logical division of labour, tight managerial control, strict accountability and clearly defined tasks and responsibilities geared to the service of "a very advanced computer system which can only work in an environment structured to the very last detail, to the very last bit - it cannot operate if there is the least departure from the rule". (An extract from the consultant's proposal for the establishment of the Division).

The People

The make-up of the staff in any organisation has a variety of effects on the climate of satisfaction. Some of the elements in the staff profile for Computer Division were significant in influencing the attitudes and reactions of the people to their work. When we arrived, there were 271 staff in post in Computer Division. The first significant feature was the age pattern, which showed that 78% of the staff were under 40 and 60% were under 30. There were more women than men overall (by 149 to 122) but the women's numbers were made up by two occupational groups - 21 junior programmers and 77 machine operators. There was only one woman at senior management level in the organisation.

The figures given to us showed that 53 people, or nearly 20% of the staff, held either a professional or a higher educational qualification of some kind. A substantial, but unquantified, additional number had experience of higher education in some form without necessarily having completed a course of study. We felt that this concentration of a high level of educational experience, coupled with the low age level, were important features. Introduced into a complex, highly structured situation was a group of people who were likely to have recent experience of fairly casual and informal systems of work organisation, who were likely to have been exposed to radical ideas and opinions and to have lived within a culture which tended to reject bureaucratic or authoritarian methods in favour of consensus and participation. We did not know to what extent the younger staff, and here we were thinking particularly of programmers and analysts, had adopted these values, but their style of dress and social behaviour suggested that, in those areas at least, there was a strong desire to preserve some element of the student lifestyle. The existence of a strong sub-culture of this kind within an organisation was clearly of importance for the way it was managed.

We used, during our researches, an instrument designed to obtain from interviewees an assessment of the main characteristics of their colleagues attitudes to work. The outcome of this research is at Figure 2. This showed that in general, people felt that their colleagues were skilled, responsible and had relatively high expectations about such things as consultation and the use to which their skills and abilities were put. Interesting variations between occupational groups showed that programmers tended to prefer a well defined job to one which was not clearly defined; and that data preparation operators

15

Figure 2   Attitude to Work Survey

	1	2	3	4	5	6	7	

A. Leaves other people to take most of the decisions on things which affect him at work.

Will protest if he is not consulted on all matters which affect him at work.

B. Capable of handling only a limited range of tasks in his job.

Capable of doing a job involving a variety of different tasks.

C. Not concerned about having social contact at work.

Regards opportunities for social contact at work as important.

D. Doesn't mind boring work.

Demands interesting work

E. Works best if the pace of the work is outside his control.

Could be given complete control over the pace of his work.

F. Needs or wants to have a well-defined job (area of operation) which he sticks to most of the time.

Works well and enjoys working in a job (area of operation) which is not clearly defined.

G. Needs to be told what to do next and how to do it.

Can organize the sequence of his work and choose the best method.

H. Unable to undertake responsibility for decisions, and take initiatives.

Able to undertake responsibility for decisions, and take initiatives.

I. Has a low level of skill and/or knowledge (expertise)

Has a high level of skill and/or knowledge (expertise)

J. Doesn't expect his skills and abilities to be used in his work.

Expects that his job will make full use of his skills and abilities.

K. Is not concerned about having job security.

Attaches high importance to job security.

L. Requires a job where continuous learning is not involved.

Can cope with a job which necessitates continuous learning (updating of knowledge).

M. Is not anxious to be promoted.

Attaches high importance to gaining promotion

N   Very concerned about salary/wages.

Attaches little importance to salary/wages.

16

were highly concerned about job security, and seemed equally divided on the question of whether they did or did not mind boring work. These differences highlighted the idea that it was probably wrong to talk about "the staff" as an integrated whole since they seemed to break up into four natural categories - programmers and analysts, data preparation staff, production staff and more senior managers - whose situation and problems were significantly different.

The Technology

An important aspect of any working environment is the technology, which in ADP does not simply involve hardware but also concerns the software and the whole technology of program writing. At the time of our investigation the computer in use was an ICL 1904A used in conjunction with the George III operating system; but this was soon to be superseded by the larger and more powerful ICL 1906S, also using the George III operating system. This switch illustrated neatly the underlying trend in many fields of government ADP work towards larger and more complex technology with the attendant need for greater specialisation amongst support staff. Thus, the George III system with its multi-programming and scheduling capability is a notable advance on previous single program systems and brings with it the need for more sophisticated and complex software and the people to understand and write it. This requirement does not stop with the specialist operation software or staff programmer, but makes its demands at all levels in the organisation; with the analyst who has to design his systems differently, and with the computer operator who finds his job substantially changed by the advent of the new hardware.

In addition, the use of various languages, standard program packages, the design of program suites and the techniques of program writing were all facets of the technology of ADP work which had an effect on the job satisfaction of ADP staff. The effect of employing programmers, often graduates, on the writing of simple utilities and coding, and the effect on them of introducing modular programming, were just two straightforward examples of the influence of software technology on job satisfaction.

The importance of this aspect of our investigation was underlined when we visited the Civil Service College and the Central Computing Agency and heard about future trends in technology - the extinction of low level languages, the formalisation of program and systems design, increased automation of program production and the increasing preponderance of large systems leading to greater demands for highly trained specialists. The ADP world will continue to experience rapid and far reaching technological changes, and the effects of these on the people involved deserve, in our view, at least as much attention and forethought as the changes themselves.

This was the basic hard data we had to go on - things which would be noted by observation and from the voluminous written material made available to us on our arrival. The soft data, the attitudes, expectations, likes and dislikes, hopes and fears of the staff were more difficult to come by and are outlined in the next chapter.

NOTES

[1]   Paul W.J. Robertson, K.B. and Herzberg, F. 'Job Enrichment pays off'
      Harvard Business Review Vol 47, 1969

3 The Staff Experience of the Organisation

The method of investigation consisted primarily of an extensive interview programme with over a hundred staff - approximately a third of the total (see Fig 3). The sample was chosen at random within each branch and grade. The interviews, which lasted anything up to two hours, were open-ended within a framework of basic questions and structured surveys, thus allowing any interesting themes that emerged to be pursued in depth. Later our provisional conclusions were submitted to a number of small groups, composed of various grades, for comment about their relevance and accuracy.

Programmers and Analysts

At their interviews programmers and analysts tended to concentrate on the impact of the new organisational structure and work procedures because these matters were uppermost in their minds. The ramifications of the new structure were having, or were anticipated as likely to have, a decisive effect on their level of job satisfaction. Five main features arose from the interviews.

    i.   Change itself

The extent of the change that Computer Division had been subjected to has already been described. The need for change from the former, more unstructured, method of working was accepted by the staff;

> "I programmed without a specification so I assumed one, and four months' work turned out to be useless."

> "Before Computer Division statisticians would specify what they wanted and it was done without any sort of a feasibility study."

> "Before Computer Division you got your specification on the back of a cigarette packet."

The actual process of introducing the new organisation, against a background of other change and inadequate staff levels, itself had created problems. The new structure had involved drawing off many of the most experienced programmers from Programming Branch to staff new branches, such as Service and Planning. Much of the expertise in particular topics went with them, so that newly constituted programming teams, deficient in managerial experience and technical ability, took on unfamiliar tasks, often inadequately documented and half completed, and found themselves trying to sort out someone else's unspecified program. Thus it is not surprising that working on "dog-end jobs" or "clearing up

Fig 3

BREAKDOWN BY GRADE AND BRANCH OF STAFF INTERVIEWED IN COMPUTER DIVISION

BRANCH	GRADE							TOTAL
	Executive					Machine Operator		
	Top Management	Senior	Middle	Junior	Clerical	Senior	Junior	
PRODUCTION	1	2	5	8	8	2	14	40
PROGRAMMING	1	2	8	19	1	-	-	31
PLANNING	2	2	2	2	-	-	-	8
SERVICE	1	1	3	1	-	-	-	6
RESOURCE	-	1	2	-	1	-	-	4
STAFF DEVELOPMENT AND STANDARDS	1	-	1	1	1	-	-	4
SURVEY	1	1	5	6	3	1	-	17
	7	9	26	37	14	3	14	110

someone else's mess" were mentioned as frequent causes of dissatisfaction among programmers. The onus for the first proper documentation of old programs was thrown onto programmers in the new teams and they sometimes complained that they did not know what was expected of them. Inevitably, target dates began to slip, and output and morale were low.

ii. Implementation of Change

The second adverse influence of change the programmers claimed was the way the new organisation was introduced, virtually over night so far as most staff were concerned, in a "big bang". One of the surveys we administered indicated that programmers were likely to protest if not consulted on matters which affect them at work, and they were certainly dissatisfied with this aspect of the original implementation of Computer Division. Though presentations were given to all levels about the new structure, they were not sufficient to satisfy a strong need for involvement, particularly at the more junior levels.

> "At the time Computer Division came into existence, there was a good deal of secrecy about the future. Staff were not informed of the new ideas. This led to a lot of rumours and a good deal of dissatisfaction."

The introduction of the new documentation standards was another often quoted example of the "bolt from the blue" method of implementing change.

> "Three volumes were dumped on my desk and I was expected to start using them straight away."

iii. The effect of the new organisation

The creation of Computer Division meant a larger, more specialised computer installation. Both these features led to problems. One of the main problems we faced in the study was trying to disentangle the inevitable tensions of organisational change from more fundamental underlying problems. It was clearly too early to make any firm judgement about the functional structure that had been introduced, yet we felt it was vital to report the staff's reaction to the new organisation and their perception of the future.

Programmers expressed fears that their job was becoming deskilled and that they were likely to become nothing more than coders, neither utilising nor developing their technical competence.

> "it is all cut and dried now - just a boring routine - almost a coding job."

21

"No decisions, and a predetermined route to take."

Many programmers did express dissatisfaction at having to do too much low level semi-coding work, though this problem was clearly not simply a result of the new organisational structure. More pertinently we found that the majority of programmers did not like the idea of rigid functional specialisation and the most experienced thought that changes to bring direct contract with user branches and to build up specific responsibilities and expertise on particular topics would strengthen personally important dimensions of the job which were being curtailed.

We tried to find out how far the new organisational structure was in fact being rigidly adhered to; and we found in practice considerable variation according to such factors as type of work and level of experience. As part of our enquiry we also asked a series of specific questions about how staff perceived the future. Whereas planners (systems analysts) saw both efficiency and motivational aspects improving, programmers - virtually without exception - expected organisational efficiency to improve, but with a substantial decline in morale and job satisfaction.

Some programmers, usually the more experienced ones, also felt they had lost an element of control and a sense of seeing the whole job through.

"We are just a cog in the wheel now."

"The structure of Computer Division has taken a lot of satisfaction away from the jobs of team leader and programmers by making lots of different bodies responsible for bits of any one job."

The increased formality and size of the organisation raised problems of co-ordination both within and between branches. Closely specifying the responsibilities of a particular branch or job can sometimes create opportunities for buck-passing, particularly when a task just falls outside the given boundaries of responsibilities or is in some way out of the ordinary. (Users commented that it was often difficult to identify anyone in Computer Division who could take a decision on a particular issue.) Whether or not people react in this way will depend very much on the extent to which they feel involved with the work and aims of the organisation, and whether there exists a sense of corporate loyalty and identity. Formality implies a move from casual and personal relationships to more structured and impersonal ones, with a possible consequent loss of a sense of personal identification with corporate tasks and goals. Though a degree of tension between branches was a deliberate design feature of the new organisation, staff recognised the trend towards a more impersonal work environment and reported that within Computer Division fences were being erected between branches and within branches which were having a divisive effect;

> "Everyone is much more territorial and bloody-minded than before."

> "You have got a scapegoat by saying the words Computer Division. Before, the onus was on you to get the work out - now the organisation is to blame. Before, you were an individual now you are just a number."

> "People do not ask 'am I doing a good job?' but they say 'am I fulfilling my terms of reference'."

Data Preparation Staff

The Data Preparation Section was subjected to no dramatic change with the introduction of the new Division - "similar people continued to do similar work". The section, which had little direct contact with other areas of the office, had two main groups, each with 24 machine operators. (These Groups used processor controlled keying equipment.) One group was engaged mainly on numeric work, the other mainly on alpha work; there was a separate miscellaneous section, and a training area; program punching on IBM card machines took place in an adjoining room. The section operated mainly as a production unit with work arriving in batches from the coding sections though there was some ad hoc work. Each operator spent about half her time punching and half verifying. The job was relatively well paid for the area and was sought after. Many of the operators joined the office because they had friends or relatives working in some other part of the building, and there was a well developed social system in the section.

At our initial meeting with the local union officials, we were asked "What can you do for the punch girls: surely they have to punch and that is that?". We were surprised to find that, though the quality of the staff seemed high, there was no great dissatisfaction with the work itself. Most of the staff had accepted the fundamental monotony of the job. There is in fact a measure of interest in the work, derived from the fact that 70% of the volumes punched are original source documents (birth, death, marriage certificates etc). What we did find was a strong reaction against people telling them "what a boring job we have" and "treating us like the dregs of the earth". Not only were they concerned with their image outside the section, but also within. "We want people to stop treating us like machines." The whole emphasis in data preparation was on "speeds up and error rate down".

This is perhaps a fairly familiar tradition in factory-like conditions where repetitive work is done, but the staff found it verging on the intolerable, and it seemed likely to be proving counter-productive. "The job is a bore, but bearable. The petty rules are unbearable."

A further aspect reinforcing the constant pressure for output at any cost was the proficiency scheme. In brief, operators had to achieve 11,000 key depressions an hour to qualify as a machine operator, and 16,000 kdph to achieve a £3 a week bonus. Each set of documents to be punched was "weighted" by means of a nationally agreed set of rules to give a notional number of depressions for any piece of work. A record of the time taken by each operator was made at the end of the week and checked against the notional key depressions. An associated factor was the measurement of error rates which had to remain below 2%. Assessment of errors depended upon the verifier reporting a colleague's errors - not surprisingly, perhaps, not many errors were reported! We found evidence that operators saw the need for some sort of incentive - this was particularly important in training, where achieving 11,000 key depressions was seen as an important goal - but the present scheme was unintelligible to the operators; this, and the problems of assessing error rates, tended to put the whole scheme into disrepute with the staff.

Though this was seen by the girls as an important incentive there was particular criticism of the over-emphasis on punching as an end in itself. For instance, some of the characters to be punched were often badly written. There used to be "a terrific system of flagging discrepancies in the work which was much more efficient". Errors were set aside and later sorted out by a coder visiting the section. The flagging system may or may not have been more efficient, but from the job satisfaction point of view, it gave operators a sense of being able to exercise some discretion. Punching work they knew to be wrong for later amendment at verification or in the edit stage, seemed a pointless exercise.

The staff felt they had no opportunity to influence the work situation, yet our brain-storming session showed that there was no lack of ideas.

"No-one has ever asked us before."

"Consultation could produce fresh ideas and more time saving methods."

There were also more personal considerations raised in the interviews. Many of the staff in data preparation had young families. Perhaps about 25% of the staff had children under ten. We found extreme concern among mothers about the difficulties of getting time off when a child was ill or had to go to the doctor. Mothers faced a real conflict of loyalty here, and felt that the organisation was unsympathetic to their predicament. Whether or not it was justified, staff felt that there was an air of disapproval from management when they asked for special leave.

"My son had to go to the optician. I could not say it was for him, so I said it was for me - a downright lie. Then everyone asked me where my glasses were."

"My son had an accident and I took him to hospital. I told the office I was sick."

The situation was such that mothers effectively took the time off but often felt that they had to resort to subterfuge to obtain it.

A number of important environmental problems causing job dissatisfaction were also reported to us. These included the fact that there was nowhere to go for a tea break - "snacks are taken at the machine and the crumbs go down the back" - the canteen was too far away and also too expensive for lunch; the taped music provided was regarded as unsuitable; the ventilation was sometimes inadequate, and the room layout could be improved.

Computer Operations Staff

Computer Operations appeared to be an area isolated from the rest of the office rather in the same way as Data Preparation. The people working there were of a distinctive type. Each shift had an identity and individuality of its own. There had been virtually no interchange between shifts, and people generally had a strong loyalty to their own group, reinforced by such factors as travelling which because of the fairly remote location led to a great dependence on lifts from others on the shift. The operating staff were in general young - appropriate for the kind of work which requires a quick and alert frame of mind, physical deftness, and some stamina. Their occasional high spirits sometimes generated problems for the older shift leaders,

"A shift leader has to be a cross between a psychologist and a prison warder!"

We found that the level of job morale and satisfaction among operation staff was relatively high, though there were reservations expressed about the future. The satisfaction was derived from the fact that many of the staff had a practical bent and a great interest in the technical aspects of the work. People not only had a varied job, but were allowed a significant amount of freedom of action.

"I like the atmosphere. You do not have people at your back; we are encouraged to take initiatives."

"I am in the driving seat of Computer Division."

There was also, inherent in the work, the satisfaction of actually producing a visible end product.

The new organisation had not had a dramatic impact on computer operators, but doubts were expressed about future changes. Each shift operated as a team. The method by which particular tasks were allocated varied according to each shift. All staff seemed to get the opportunity, not only of looking after the peripherals, but also operating the console which was one of the most sought after jobs. The supervisor's job was to oversee these activities and to ensure that the machine and peripherals were operated at maximum efficiency. This involved deciding, for instance, in what order the schedule should be run. The overriding fear we found among these staff was that their job was likely to be devalued when the new computer arrived. The new machine would operate with two shifts which would mean more staff on shift. The new computer room was much larger and this would mean people would be dispersed around the area and would no longer be able to congregate in a friendly group around the console. There would be a need for changes in floor organisation. The machine would run faster which would mean increased physical work in handling tapes. These factors in isolation might be acceptable, but the staff also thought that many of the interesting aspects of the work would be removed. For instance, the more sophisticated George 3 system would take over the supervisor's scheduling function. These supervisors feared they would lose much of the managerial content of their job and become console operators only.

"I have been running a shift for three years and now I am back to console operating."

Most junior operators believed they would no longer be allowed to operate the computer.

"Pride for us will be decreased because we will do no operating."

The machine operators believed they would become porters, machine minders and cleaners as more rigid specialisation began to creep in.

We found in the operating area, rather as in the programming area, that people felt that they were losing control of their work. They had already experienced this phenomonem to some extent in the switch to a more sophisticated operating system (George II to George III) and the trend seems likely to continue as more sophisticated systems emerge from manufacturers. The technological influences were a good deal stranger than the effects of the new organisation in the computer room.

"We are losing control in the computer room. Before, we knew what was happening - now its all done by George!"

"The machine is running you."

The development of a more instrumental attitude to work because of technological progress was perceived by many, but was apparently unstoppable.

An example of this inexorable trend was the feasibility study on the introduction of terminals for program development work in Computer Division. This stated;

"Computer operating staff regard the transfer of computing tasks to programmers at terminals as an erosion of their area of responsibility; they consider that their function is in the process of relegation from computer operating to machine minding. Operator job satisfaction is therefore likely to be somewhat impaired, with the strong likelihood of a concomitant loss of morale."

What was of concern to us was that the study went on to say that it considered the effects on morale to be inherent in the evolution of an increasingly versatile operating system. We found this assumption of inevitability a worrying one, and we return to it later in Chapter 15.

Computer operators felt that they were poor relations so far as promotion opportunities went. On our very first visit, the operators showed us a magazine article which described the relatively low status level that operators are accorded generally in spite of the considerable responsibility they have and the value of the equipment they handle. The implications of the article were that they would have to help themselves if they wanted career advancement. This contrasted fairly sharply with the promotion pattern for programmers with whom there was some degree of tension,

"Programers think we are a lot of numbleweeds."

"The supervisors shift stay for years and block promotion for us. Then when one goes, a person of any equivalent grade may be brought in from right outside Computer Division altogether."

In spite of these comments and doubts an important feature was that virtually no-one wanted to leave the computer operations environment even on promotion, because this would mean a loss of the shift payment. These staff were perhaps the most contented in the Division though some computer operators felt that there was a lack of consultation about matters which affected them at work. Though there had been improvements in internal communications one frequently recurring comment concerned the introduction of two shift working where consultation had been insufficient. The unions had been asked for their comments, certainly, and management did consult the staff, but at a stage when people felt that decisions had already been made.

Survey Branch

Survey Branch provided us with an interesting example of a unit with working methods and management style very different to anything else we had come across. Though the branch was part of Computer Division, it was located in

27

London. We were aware that this organisational link had been, at the time of its creation, a topic of great concern to the staff of Survey Branch. They had seen it as a threat to their usual methods of working - in close touch with Research Officers and being involved with a project from a very early stage through to its completion. They had also feared a relocation. The inclusion of Survey Branch in Computer Division had in fact brought none of these things, but there was some concern among the staff about the future.

Job satisfaction and morale was generally at a high level in Survey Branch and we attributed it to four main factors:

   i.   The small size of the branch;

   ii.   The methods of working which involve close contact and detailed involvement with most stages of a project;

   iii.   Work which was intrinsically interesting for people who had chosen social survey work because they were interested in this field and were also able to pursue interests in computing and methodology;

   iv.   A style of management which was generally democratic, informal and allowed staff a good degree of autonomy in their work.

We felt that the majority of the staff were very content with the existing working situation, organisation and location. However we detected a fairly strong undercurrent of concern about the future among many of the staff we talked to. They were anxious to preserve their informal, semi-autonomous methods of working but saw this being threatened by future developments over which they had little control, eg

   i.   The considerable growth in the size of the branch as extra staff were taken on to run the new terminal, and as more senior posts were created to take on new areas of work,

   ii.   The increased reliance on the rest of Computer Division that would come with the installation of the new terminal linked to the newly installed ICL 1906S and the phasing out of the use of the IBM Bureau.

Things were clearly not going to go on as they had before and the staff had already noted a trend towards more formal methods of administration within the branch. Some staff saw this as the thin end of a bureaucratic wedge which would inevitably become more intrusive as the branch grew bigger. There were certainly signs that the old informal methods were becoming strained. In many ways the rather insidious development of more bureaucratic traits was a reflection of what was happening to Computer Division as a whole. It was also a reflection of the sort of social developments we referred to in the opening chapter.

4 The Broad Themes of the Diagnosis

When we had completed our programme of interviews and had studied the material we had gathered, some broad issues began to emerge in our minds. To check that we had identified the correct and important issues and to explore them in more depth, we held a series of group meetings - some with staff drawn from particular areas or branches, others with a cross section of staff from the whole Division. Three themes emerged fairly clearly from this series of meetings. They concerned:

The style of management

The functioning of the organisation

The implementation and management of change.

None of these stood on its own and there was a close inter-relationship between them. They seemed to us to provide an appropriate focus for any future initiatives and we adopted them as the central themes for our report.

The style of management is a rather nebulous concept. We have described how staff at lower levels felt they were denied a chance to influence or participate in the making of decisions. The evidence of the surveys supported this view, but it also showed that there was a question of degree. The diagnosis was most marked in Programming Branch, where the demand for participation was strident yet where the style of management was already relatively informal. The feelings also existed in Data Preparation, where the demand was less strong but where the regime was more authoritarian. In various forms and to varying degrees, the demand was present right through the organisation - and we even came across signs of it in Survey Branch which, on the face of it, was managed in quite a democratic way.

There was also the question of the level at which, and the way in which, the demand became manifest. It was certainly present at those levels in the organisation which had no managerial responsibility of their own such as the junior programmers and the machine operators in Data Preparation. But it was also present, in a slightly different form, at higher levels. Some programming section leaders, for instance, felt that they were not involved by those above them in important decision making; because of rapid promotion, inexperience and, in a few cases, immaturity, some felt unable to manage their teams in the way that, as first line managers, they should, and some complained of not really knowing what was expected of them.

We felt too that a consuming interest in the technology and techniques of ADP work had a tendency to relegate questions of management style to a position of lesser importance in the minds of managers at all levels.

In respect of the second of our themes, the functioning of the organisation, we were rather hamstrung by the undertaking we had given when we first arrived not to propose any changes in the structure of the organisation, since it was a relatively new one. However we did say that we would raise warning signals concerning any human issues that arose from its structure or functioning. It soon became clear to us that there were indeed problems connected with the way in which the organisation was, or was not, working which raised issues affecting morale. Problems of communication across branch boundaries were particularly remarked on. Some of these were the sort of troubles that will arise with the running-in of any new organisation. Others were closely linked to the operation of the documentation standards, which were said not to be fulfilling their function of defining "the ingredients of communications about concepts, products or plans ...... essential to the instructions of work to be carried out by Computer Division staff" (Consultants "Proposals" for the establishment of Computer Division): as a result, staff were finding their work full of frustration, uncertainty and ambiguity. Other communication problems were probably due to sheer human cussedness.

What struck us strongly was that there was no formal machinery for identifying and remedying these problems other than by going to a senior managerial level, where often the informal "old boy" network was brought into play to get things done, which might not always be the best or most efficient way of doing things. By contrast, one particular initiative had been taken by staff in the training branch, who, perceiving a problem of this kind, set up on their own initiative a training activity, followed by a round table meeting of interested parties at junior level to thrash out the problems. Eventually, a report was produced which was given a wide distribution to all branch heads. This initiative was viewed by some managers as an attempt to usurp their role and in the event the follow up was protracted, and a good deal of the impetus and enthusiasm of the staff was dissipated as a result. This incident illustrated clearly to us the advantages to be gained, both for efficiency and morale by encouraging and making use of the experience and abilities of staff at all levels in the identification, investigation and remedying of organisational malfunctions. It also demonstrated the potential of the training staff for fulfilling this role of identifying organisational difficulties and co-ordinating activities of this sort.

It was obvious that the functioning of an organisation had implications for relationships outside its boundaries as well as inside. We felt that there was a great deal of concern among staff about the reputation of the Division with its customers and the resulting quality of the working relationship between them and their contacts in the user divisions. There was a natural distaste at having to listen to criticisms from users of delays and short-comings in service; there was a feeling that Computer Division had been oversold, and that the consultants had underestimated the problems of setting up the organisation. It was felt that more could be done to make users aware of the reasons for the shortfall in performance, and that the Division should put its own house in order and clear the backlog of work before entering into any more substantial commitments with the user divisions.

The final theme concerned the management of change. One of the chief lessons to be drawn from the early experience was the crucial importance of managing the implementation of change of all kinds with foresight and sensitivity. Whether the innovation was the introduction of a new time sheet for data preparation work, the creation of the new operating standards or the installation of a new computer there were effects, short and long term, on the people involved, both as individuals and as members of working groups. We found that there was an awareness among staff at all levels of impending changes, of the effect that these changes would have on them and a desire on the part of the staff for a chance to contribute in a constructive way to the planning and implementation of these changes. People wanted to do a good job. On the whole, participation of this kind had not happened in the past, and the results of our investigation suggested there was a strong desire for improvement in this direction.

One example which illustrates this was the behaviour of a small team reporting on the implications of installing terminals. They obtained views on the effects of such terminals on the work and job satisfaction of programmers and computer operators at several outside installations and referred to them in their feasibility study report. Yet we found that neither programmers nor computer operators in Computer Division were asked specifically for their comments. Thus the report reflected views held in outside organisations, but not grass roots opinion at the location where the terminals were about to be installed!

We felt we had identified the right themes, but how we were to present them to the office, and, even more crucially, what might be done about them, now became major problems for us.

5 A Programme for Change

It had been an important underlying assumption of our diagnostic work from an early stage that, although our primary aim was to "let the people speak for themselves", we also had a duty to be analytic about the information we were providing. Thus, although we might report, as we did, that programmers felt that they would work better in cellular (as opposed to open plan) offices, that data preparation girls felt they needed longer and more frequent breaks, or that Planning and Control staff felt that they needed more training - all of which were true and would improve job satisfaction - we formed a judgement that these were not problems of fundamental importance. They were, we felt, symptomatic of another deeper issue which was of much greater significance for the long term effectiveness and health of the organisation and for the development and satisfaction of those who worked in it. It seemed to us that the basic problems was a fundamental mismatch between, on the one hand, the organisational style and managerial regime that existed in the Division, and, on the other, the expectations and abilities of the staff. To caricature the situation a little, but only a little, we were watching a tightly structured organisation designed with all the practices and principles of scientific management in mind in which tasks were minutely described so as to avoid any ambiguity or uncertainty and where managers' duties and responsibilities were rigorously defined and tied very closely to the traditional hierarchy of the Civil Service, trying to absorb the talented and able products of an educational system and society where questioning and enquiring behaviour were encouraged, where attitudes to authority were changing rapidly and where the prevailing values were to do with consensus, democracy and the need for self-expression - and where some of the Managers had quite as much sympathy with their younger colleagues as with the system!

Our main problem therefore was to try to decide on a set of proposals which would be recognised as feasible, practical and operational whilst at the same time tackling not the surface problems but the major problem of the mismatch of attitudes and values. A fundamental readjustment of the kind that we considered necessary was not something that was going to be achieved by a little organisational tinkering, sensitivity training or job enrichment. We were looking for means of reducing the basic contradiction of organisational principles and social and educational values that existed within the office. We were looking for a process that would integrate these disparate aspects of working life in a way that would be acceptable to all and which would mean that no one group would have to make unilateral concessions to another.

Already in the diagnosis three important themes had emerged and were likely to provide an appropriate focus for any further activity - the style of management, the functioning of the organisation and the implementation and management of change; added to this was the strong dissatisfaction with the lack

32

of opportunity to participate in or influence day-to-day working decisions in the division. We felt that if this mixture of the desire to modify the style of management, particularly in regard to the management of change, the desire to improve the way the organisation was functioning and the strong under-current of the need for more participation could be mobilised and given expression through a practical process it would prove a potent force for resolving the contradiction in the organisation and developing a better and more healthy working environment for the future. The key was the underlying desire for participation which we saw both as the expression of the need for a better dialogue and a demand for more opportunities for self-expression on the part of most of the younger staff. A style of management genuinely founded on the principle of direct participation would, we felt, create the kind of working environment in which many of the other problems and issues could be resolved and in which the elements of the mismatch could be unified in a common pursuit.

These rather imprecise, philosophical and perhaps idealistic ideas had to be given expression in a practical and realistic set of proposals which could be understood and which had a chance of being accepted by the hardworking and down to earth managers, union officials and staff. What eventually emerged, therefore, was a program of development which was based on the premise that, although the original creation and setting to work of the organisation had been a major step forward in providing an effective computing service for the Department, what was now needed was a program of interlinked development work at different levels and in different areas of the organisation which could be seen as an important and necessary second step in developing this service. The aims of the program would be:

1. To achieve a growing willingness amongst all levels of managers to consult their staff before decisions which affected them at work were made.

2. To create a climate in which appropriate decision making responsibility could be delegated to every level in the organisation.

3. To employ to the full the accumulated knowledge, experience and expertise of all staff in the development of an effective and responsive organisation.

4. To help staff at all levels to prepare themselves for, and cope with, the changes that these developments would produce.

A Program for Organisation Development

It was important that any process of development to be embarked upon in Computer Division should build on the foundations already laid. Furthermore,

33

the process itself should be evolutionary, starting from relatively small beginnings in order to stand a chance of being self-sustaining as it grew in scope. The program would be task and problem oriented, and we would expect to see it develop along the following lines. The stages were not necessarily in chronological order; for instance the third and fourth stages might with advantage be initiated in parallel with the first and second.

First Stage This would centre around a series of meetings within each branch, involving staff from all levels, aimed at identifying specific operational issues and problems interfering with the efficient working of the branch.

It would be important, having once decided on an agenda of issues and problems, to concentrate in discussion, not on what the solution should be, although some guidelines and advice could be drawn from the meeting, but on which individual or group should be responsible for seeking a solution and implementing it, and what consultation (up, down and sideways) should precede any implementation.

These early attempts could well be rather long-winded and difficult for all concerned. For this reason we thought it important for the meetings to be attended, although not run, by an external agent (or consultant) whose role would be to comment on the process and to pursue, with individuals and groups, any problems that arose.

To begin with it would be sensible to concentrate on straightforward problems, capable of relatively easy solution, so that confidence in the process could be quickly gained. Later, matters of more weight could be handled in the same way. In this way the proper levels for decision making within a branch would be established, the knowledge and expertise within the branch would be properly used and staff would feel a greater sense of involvement in the decision making process.

Second Stage This would begin when the solution of problems in one branch began to effect activities in another. It would become necessary to consider how the process could be extended to allow examination of divisional as well as branch problems.

Some kind of machinery would be needed to handle this, and we believed that the Staff Development Branch was in a unique position within Computer Division to identify and investigate organisational problems. As the training branch it had a wide view of the operation of the division, as branch responsible for the ADP documentation standards it had the key responsibility for ensuring the smooth working of the communication network, and as branch responsible for career development it received a good deal of information about all aspects of the organisation's human activities. This combination of factors suggested to us that the role of the branch should be more interventionist, seeking out organisational weakness and developing, with the staff directly involved,

34

solutions and remedies. This would give a much more positive flavour to the "staff development" aspect of its task and would in fact be building on initiatives already taken in that branch. Again, the details would have to be worked out with some care, and a start on a small scale would be indicated. The external agent would need to be closely involved with the development of a new role for Staff Development Branch although his role would be to advise on the process of the development and he would take no direct part in the actual identification and solution of organisational problems.

Third Stage We had already suggested that these participative methods of management could be stressful, particularly to managers who were living under considerable pressure of day-to-day work. Thus a necessary adjunct to the development of these methods would be some assistance for the managers in Computer Division (particularly the branch heads in the first place), to help them as individuals and as a team to adapt to developments and cope with the new demands they would make on them. This would best come from a consultant experienced in this kind of work. The nature of the assistance would depend very much on the style of the consultant, the particular needs of the management team and the demands of the developing situation, so it was not possible to spell out in any great detail at that stage what would be involved.

Fourth Stage Another area where special attention was merited was Data Preparation. Here, a kind of persistent managerial mythology about the awfulness of the job and the hopelessness of improving it had, we believed, prevented any real attempt to improve conditions. This attitude was widespread throughout the Civil Service and was reinforced in official publications where the accent was heavily on the technical rather than the human side of the problems, staff management considerations being given only passing attention. Even unions seemed to expect little to be achieved in the area. And on the surface it was a difficult problem. We had a dominant technology and a work situation comparable to factory production work. With a given technology and a continuous throughput of repetitive, short-cycle work, the scope for operators to take decisions and exercise discretion about their work was inevitably limited; but it had been made even more so by the managerial methods adopted. We detected some important signs during our study that suggested a potentially productive way forward. There seemed to be a lively and widespread group spirit; there was a great deal of experience and knowledge of the process among the staff; and there was an eagerness to make suggestions and to discuss them logically and positively. We felt that these could be developed within the framework of an experimental group, the lessons from which might well be applicable more generally within the data preparation area.

The proposal was to take a group of staff with their supervisor and to develop with them at group meetings a list of suggestions and proposals for improving the management of their task. Then, jointly with management and staff, the feasibility and methods of implementation of these changes would be discussed before they were put into effect. From the evidence of our interviews with data preparation staff the list of changes could cover a wide spectrum and might well include topics under all of the following headings:

the amount of work to be done in a period;

the sequencing and flow of work;

the allocation of work within the group;

the processing of queries;

the verification of work;

acceptable error rates;

the time taken for breaks;

the working environment.

To avoid too much dislocation of production it would be necessary to conduct a strictly limited experiment with one group of staff to begin with.

Implications of the Programme

The implications of such a programme were clearly wide ranging. In general it was clear that if our proposals were implemented they could involve a great deal of change which, though gradual, could be stressful for all concerned. Staff at lower levels would experience more responsibility for decision making. Managers would be asked to delegate more authority, experiencing the element of judgement and risk-taking that this involved; they would also be seeking and adopting new roles within the organisation. Experience in other job satisfaction work of this kind had shown that the ambiguity and uncertainty that this created could be painful and stressful at first, though intensely rewarding in the long run.

All the initiatives outlined required the assistance of at least one outsider or third party. Resources from within the organisation would also be needed. It followed therefore that all these proposals could not be put in hand together. In any case we viewed the whole programme as part of an evolutionary process which would grow from fairly small beginnings, probably the internal branch meetings to begin with, although we thought it would be important to involve the Training and Staff Development Branch and commence the managerial development work at a fairly early stage as well.

At first glance the prospect of a regular series of protracted meetings attended by staff at all levels in the division seemed likely to threaten output and productivity. Experience in other offices had shown however that productivity,

36

as measured by all conventional indicators, need not suffer. We argued that commitment of time to this sort of activity was an investment in increased future effectiveness and was an essential part of the "second major step forward" which must now follow the creation of the administrative machinery of Computer Division.

The natural conclusion of this programme would be the self sustaining process in which all the aims outlined above were being fulfilled. It was clearly not possible to forecast with certainty how long this would take, but comparable programmes had produced encouraging and valuable results after about six months.

The least tangible of the implications of this kind of programme was the degree of support and commitment a programme of this kind would earn from management and the Unions (or Staff Side, as the collective role of the Unions is termed in civil service parlance). We felt that "earn" was probably the operative word, since it would be naive to expect unequivocal support and co-operation until the benefits of what was being proposed were demonstrated. Nevertheless, without an initial agreement from both management and Unions to suspend judgement and participate, a programme like this could not get off the ground at all. This was the kind of commitment that would be sought to begin with - a willingness to defer reaching a verdict. This might not be easy while managers were being asked to take risks and delegate authority, and the Unions might see some of their traditional status and authority being "eroded" - but without an initial open minded commitment the chances of success would be greatly diminished.

It was clear that if this programme were allowed to develop there would come a time, probably sooner rather than later, when the relationship of the Division with the rest of the Office would be questioned or affected in some way. What form this would take was not easy to forecast, but containment of a process of this kind might be very difficult and a rather artificial constraint on its development; we felt that all concerned should be aware of this important implication and what was being suggested.

We had stressed that the kind of development programme we were proposing was a "second major step" towards the creation of an effective computing service for the office. This put sharply into focus what we saw to be the relative importance of the human, material and organisational aspects of such an undertaking. Setting up the structure and installing the hardware were essential first steps in the process, but without attention to the human dimension the organisation would remain lifeless and inert. The "second major step" was therefore the one which made the organisation work, and work effectively. Our contribution was to help management and staff to tap abilities and ideas which too often lay dormant. We argued that the release of these talents helped to produce organisations which were effective and satisfying to work in, where staff contributed to the successful management of the task and felt a sense of ownership of the developing system to which they had contributed.

We were aware that our proposals were rather simplistic and that there was a great deal more to what we were proposing than appeared in the report. The aim was to achieve changes in behaviour and attitudes through a participative process, but much depended on the way people perceived what was being attempted, whether they were willing and able to learn from what was going on and what the effect would be on the political nature of organisational life and on the concentration of power within the division.

6 The Reservations of Management

In Chapter 4 we discussed the broad themes that emerged from our diagnostic exercise;

> the style of management,

> the functioning of the organisation,

> the implementation and management of change.

It was the first theme that we concentrated on simply because the others are necessarily subordinate to it. With a new style of management it would be possible to modify the other issues by an evolutionary process. The approach thus differed from more traditional methods of consultancy because, potentially, it did allow the interested individual to advance his views and influence the decisions which affected him and his work.

It is worth explaining just what we meant by different style of management. We believed that it would mean that managers at all levels would need to allow some forum where more junior staff could put their ideas up for consideration. It would mean delegating real authority on appropriate issues for decisions to be made at more junior levels - not just a cosmetic consultation process, "agreement with my views after suitable discussion". This in turn implied appropriate information would be made available and the necessary time would be given. It would mean managers talking more openly and frankly to all people involved. It would mean listening to what staff at all levels were saying and respecting their point of view. Our task was to begin to develop these attitudes in the organisation generally, and to create an environment where the employee felt that it was worthwhile to contribute.

We returned to Computer Division some four months after our investigation in order to discuss our findings with management and unions. Two features struck us forcibly.

A number of initiatives had already been taken by the managers which went some way towards our ideas. The most interesting example was the establishment of a task force of relatively junior staff to examine documentation standards. This demonstrated the possibilities of the approach which we had advocated in our report. Though these initiatives had been on a rather ad hoc basis they were encouraging. They implied a recognition that Computer Division did need an involved and committed staff and would not automatically settle down and run like a machine. Though encouraging, these initiatives had not sufficient momentum to solve the problems. They were too isolated and lacked a coherent strategy and had not generally caught the imagination of the staff. We doubted that there would be more progress without a climate more conducive to development.

The second feature was the considerable discussion at all levels, but particularly at top management level, about the most appropriate form of organisational structure for Computer Division. There were several points of view on this issue among the managers but the very fact that such informal discussions were taking place surprised us. When we had first come to the office it had been made clear to us that it was an inappropriate time to consider organisational change. We now found considerable feeling that such change might be necessary. We wondered whether the managers fears concerning more organisational change were any less valid then than earlier. We were convinced that organisational changes of themselves would not solve the problems. The key lay, we believed, in an evolutionary process which would permit the organisation to adapt gradually and continually to change as it occurred rather than moving from one major upheaval to the next. When we began to discuss the diagnosis with senior management we found that it was less than enthusiastically received and various criticisms were levelled at us. One of the managers wondered if in fact we were seeking solutions to problems that did not exist. Objective measures such as staff turnover and absenteeism did not appear to be particularly significant and though productivity was apparently low this could be possibly explained by the extent of the change the division had recently undergone. The argument that "the problem does not exist" reflects the difficulty in making the jump from interpreting the behaviour and attitudes one observes and reports, and relating it to specific problems and solutions. "Climate" in an organisation is a nebulous and intangible concept and because of this, suggestions for improvement based, apparently, on a series of group meetings appeared less than convincing.

A general criticism of the managers and union officers which summed up our immediate problem was that the report had not matched people's expectations in that it did not contain specific recommendations for action apart from "a lot of group meetings". We realised then that we had in fact failed to get over the essential message that we were suggesting a developmental process for the organisation, rather than delivering specific solutions. A developmental process by definition rules out a specifically pre-determined outcome.

We were criticised for bias towards the staff's views and failing to put forward the management side. Our diagnostic report was in fact a reflection of the staffs' perspective, simply reporting their subjective views of their situation. We argued that this approach was quite defensible for its strength was that although it might appear to be unbalanced, it was about reality as experienced by the staff. Another comment was that we were attempting to introduce participation in which staff would not really be interested as long as managers kept them informed of what was going on. A variation of this was that the staff would be so interested it might lead to anarchy! Certainly it was thought that the data preparation girls would not be interested in any form of participation and we were accused of projecting middle class values onto them. A final shot was that though we had identified continuous change as a major problem we were ourselves recommending a further period of instability.

We recognised that a pre-requisite for launching a project aimed at achieving a change in management style was to get a commitment for some sort of activity. At the end of the first meeting there was a rather reluctant and confused agreement that we could return to the Division to develop and discuss our ideas, but there was no mention of implementation.

The period of four weeks during which these discussions continued was the most difficult of the project. There was a feeling of being personna non grata in the organisation. It was not that people were any less friendly but having not properly digested our findings they were unsure what was expected of them and found the ambiguity of the situation stressful. The managers believed that having cooperated fully in the study they had done their bit and would like to get on with their work. The staff were not overjoyed with the report. It was considered by most to be a non event in that it did not openly propose specific radical change nor was it openly critical of management. They did not really believe anything would come of it. The unions no less than management found the philosophy difficult to grasp in practical terms and made some rather superficial comments. All in all we appear to have fallen between two stools, satisfying neither the hawks nor the doves. We set ourselves the task during this period of sounding out in detail the reservations of the managers and trying to discuss them. We also wished to spell out the philosophy of the approach we were advocating in greater detail and to consider some of the practical issues concerned with the implementation of our ideas.

Reservations about Participation

Various issues were raised in these discussions with the managers and are worth elaborating on as a prelude to the events of the project.

Some managers feared that the development of a participative type of organisation might detract from their managerial authority. They thought that participation might possibly lead to a chaotic situation with many groups having to be involved in all decisions. We explained that this was not what a participative approach was likely to bring about. Normal line management was unlikely to be usurped, nor would all decisions be appropriate for consideration by groups at junior levels. Line managers would still have to manage but in a different way. We explained that we thought that tapping the source of talent at junior levels would call for managerial leadership of a high order, the challenge of which was likely to provide enhanced job satisfaction for senior managers.

Some managers expressed some doubts about the role of the external consultant and the role of any internal third party who might be drawn from within the organisation. For instance they expressed concern that there might be

41

some interference in the internal affairs of their branches. It was important for us to stress that the third party would not be involved in identifying which problems should be tackled. The job of the third party would primarily be to assist with the inter-branch problem. His role would include,

Attending group meetings.

Following up and helping resolve points of conflict.

Arranging communication of data deriving from meetings.

Providing a link with higher management and Staff Side.

We also explained we would consider it important that a senior manager, preferably in the training field, from within the Division should be appointed to work with us and help service the project. He would remain responsible for the project after we departed.

There were management doubts about whether or not a more participative approach would work. We could only say that on the basis of the evidence it appeared to be a sensible and appropriate strategy and we believed that the situation in the Division was conducive to this type of approach. Of course we were not able to guarantee success - there was an element of risk and learning in the whole process. By definition, one started off by not knowing the final outcome. We explained that we were convinced that staff at a junior level would respond to trust in a responsible way, that they did want to do a good job and would demonstrate this if given the opportunity.

A further point concerned the time which would be required by staff for group activities. We explained that we thought the time involved was unlikely to be more than an hour or two a week for each group. In other organisations it had been found that staff had developed a commitment to the process of greater involvement and had been able to "find the time" without any fall off in the usual performance measures kept by the office.

There was also anxiety about the methods of working. How would the problems be identified? We pointed out that already in our absence managers had initiated a number of group meetings which had identified specific problems. We explained that the results of the group discussions would seem to confirm that there was a considerable degree of untapped knowledge and experience in the organisation. We thought that priority could be allocated to the problems identified and the particular manager or managers involved could set up groups with the help of the third party to consider and report on the problems. The responsibility for implementation of further action could be delegated, if it was appropriate to do so, to suitable groups. We explained that participation did not mean management by abdication. Work groups of this type would ask the more senior managers for help with problems they themselves

42

could not handle, calling in the particular experience and expertise of managers where they thought it necessary. Higher management would thus operate in a supportive rather than a directive role, responding to the needs as they arose. Management would have more time to focus on the policy, planning and longer term issues which were essential to the success of the office.

A final worry concerned the impact the implementation of participative management might have on the accepted union relationships in the organisation. We explained that we did not expect participative management to diminish the role of the staff representatives. However, if staff themselves were experiencing real participation in their day to day working it was likely their official representatives would find there was a need to be more truly representative than might have been necessary in the past. Similarly, management might find itself working more intimately with staff and staff representatives. There was thus a sense in which the process was likely to improve the official dialogue between management and unions just as it was likely to make normal everyday working relationship more productive and meaningful.

After a month of these further discussions it was clear to us that the talking had to stop. Having been through these issues with management and in the process having identified some significant problems in the top management team itself, we explained that we thought a debate needed to take place at top management level away from the everyday office environment. If management could resolve their difficulties and decide on a united plan for achieving their organisational objectives with more openness among themselves this would provide a climate in which the initiatives already made could lead to a more coherent strategy.

We therefore proposed that the most useful function we could undertake at that stage was to set up a workshop for top management over a period of three days where managers would be able to give these issues the consideration they required. The theme of the workshop would be "achieving our organisational aims in the future". It would include discussion of initiatives already taken, organisational problems and future options.

7 The Managers Agree: the Worthing Workshop

The reasons for proposing the workshop and for its being accepted are probably worth examining in some detail. We are clear now that this intervention became, fortuitously, the breakthrough that we had been looking for. As to why it was suggested, it was simply just about the only thing that we could think of to break the impasse that faced us. It was, as an experienced colleague commented, a "high risk" venture, but the risks involved were, we considered, worth taking. Interestingly, managers later told us that they did not see it in this light at all. They "welcomed and looked forward to it as an opportunity to sort things out". As to why the suggestion was accepted the reasons are not clear. Obviously, a combination of factors helped to prepare the ground. For instance:

i.   the "threat" of an imminent report from the external manpower audit team;

ii.   the "evolutionary approach" we were proposing was seen as a counter to the threat of imposed change which might stem from this report;

iii. the managers had delayed taking a considered view on our report and looked on the workshop as an ideal opportunity to develop such a view;

iv.   personal ambition and desire for change and improvement on the part of several of the managers was also an important factor;

v.   our low key approach, and its emphasis on building relationships rather than pushing solutions, was perhaps not regarded as threatening by the managers;

vi.   recent publicity about job satisfaction work in the press and in Civil Service publications may have excited some interest;

vii. there were real and apparently intractable problems facing the managers, some of whom were not satisfied by the piecemeal way they had been attempting to tackle them; they were being offered an opportunity to make a concerted approach.

We were not present when the managers met to consider the paper in which we had made our proposals, but we were told afterwards that despite some opposition the majority of the managers were in favour of the idea. This decision opened the door to a year's fascinating, frustrating and ultimately highly rewarding work. We had already suggested possible dates for the workshop to be

44

held at a hotel in Worthing. How to organise or structure a session of this kind required serious consideration. In discussion with colleagues in our team and at the Civil Service College we identified six features which we would build into the design of the workshop. These were;

> first, there would be some pre-course preparation by the managers;

> second, we would contract for the first few hours to be given to us so that we could mount some initial team building exercises;

> third, the agenda for the rest of the three days, and the allocation of the time, should be entirely in the manager's own hands, except that;

> fourth, we would also provide a guest speaker for one evening session to talk on issues related to job satisfaction and participation in the Civil Service;

> fifth, we would ensure that an efficient and rapid secretarial service would be provided and;

> sixth, we would make the strong point that some kind of communique or report back to the office as a whole would be prepared.

The first task was to ask each manager to write a short summary of his reactions to three basic questions - has the organisation operated as envisaged; what problems do the staff perceive; how have we (the top management group) operated as a team? This provided a veritable goldmine of thoughtful comment and opinion which not only gave us a good view about where the division stood, but also provided the managers themselves with what was perhaps their first concerted look at the operation of the division since it had come into being. Quotations must inevitably be selective, but the following give a flavour of the kinds of issues being raised in answer to each of the questions.

"Has the organisation operated as envisaged?"

> "In that the organisation was devised to provide adequately for all the computing needs of the office, it has not. Or perhaps I should say, not yet."

> "There is considerable resistance to the "bureaucracy" which Computer Division has attempted to impose (budgets, terms of business, quotas etc etc).

> The division's aura of super efficiency has proved impossible to maintain and caused resentment at all levels."

"(Staff in senior posts in the Division) ... were obliged to carry out procedures which they had had no opportunity to influence. The radical and sudden changes in work patterns and the large volume of on-going work which could not be operated under the new procedures, generated a sense of frustration and low morale."

"Too many Computer Division branches with need to know a topic in detail; tendency towards bureaucracy."

"Loss of confidence in organisation by staff."

"More important is the lack of a co-ordinated approach which raises questions about the way we are running the division and perhaps about the structure itself."

"I feel the answer must be no. The organisation has not operated as envisaged ...... Staff coming from a project-orientated environment find it difficult to adjust to a functional organisation and felt they had not been sufficiently consulted in its formation, as far as they were concerned it had been imposed on them."

"What problems do the staff perceive?"

"The key issue I think is a feeling of a lack of involvement by people in the overall objectives of the projects on which they are working."

"The interface between Branches, at all levels"

"Ignorance of job boundaries, other people's and their own."

"Lack of feeling of responsibility at all levels. Lack of motivation."

"Staff . . . feel that their contribution is more limited than it should be . . . . In nearly all cases, they see the need for change directed towards providing more individual responsibility and authority within Computer Division for getting particular projects implemented or for dealing with the whole of a particular customer's work."

"How have we operated as a team?"

"Some differences in opinion or approach have gone on too long underlying discussions between managers where it would have been better to bring the differences to the surface and resolve them. I feel that there has not been enough willingness to entrust responsibilities to each other . . ."

"Conflicts between the branch heads have caused some ill feeling. Differences of opinion as to the proper role of some branches and posts have proved impossible to reconcile."

"Recently I have noted more discussion between branch managers and a sense of greater togetherness and a wish to make things work."

"Generally speaking, managers have been so involved in the day to day operations of their branches, against a background of delay and criticism, that they have had little opportunity to stand back and look at the wider issues."

"Pressures to get work done have resulted in the triggering of the automatic defence measure of blaming everyone else for delays without looking inwards. A change of attitude would help in some instances. If the organisation is to succeed then there is the need for the will for this to happen."

"We listened to the progress reports at management meetings defending our own "patch" as need be. We certainly did not act as a team. Of late, this situation has been changing I feel we have all come to realise that many of Computer Division's problems cross branch boundaries and need to be resolved by branch managers acting together."

"With hindsight I feel Computer Division lost a great deal of momentum when the consultants left, not because they set up the organisation but because, although they acted as branch managers, they were a team; they met at lunchtime, and in the evenings and resolved problems together, not in isolation. The situation is changing, I feel for the better, and I would like to see the gradual change taking place encouraged. We need to act together more as a team and to hold more open discussions on the problems facing Computer Division and to ensure that the appropriate action is taken to resolve them".

These comments, we felt more than justified the diagnosis we had made and set the scene for what we hoped would be a lively and fruitful three day workshop.

The second feature, the manager's ownership of the agenda was fairly simply achieved. A list of key issues was circulated amongst the managers for comment, and at one of their regular management meetings a list of topics was agreed;

- organisational objectives and structure of Computer Division

- job satisfaction and the management of Computer Division

47

and under each heading five or six key questions were asked. The managers also agreed that a firm agenda would be left until after the opening session and agreed to spend the first evening session in devising the agenda for the following two days.

The third feature, our own input to the session, caused us most of the headaches. The aim was to offer some basic team building activities on the first afternoon to break the ice and to create a better working atmosphere. We used two well known exercises - Moonshot" and the "Belbin" analysis of team member roles. Briefly, Moonshot is a simple exercise the aim of which is to rank a list of items in order of importance to a hypothetical astronaut stranded on the moon; the exercise illustrates the difference between individual and group decision making and emphasises the need for compromise and co-operation in working as a group. The Belbin analysis was devised by the Industrial Training Research Unit at Cambridge under the direction of Dr Meredith Belbin and is used to identify the skills and different role characteristics needed to achieve a balanced management team. It depends on the structured analysis of each individual in a group by his colleagues and was used in this case not to illustrate any particular imbalance in the team but to provide some self knowledge for individual members of the team, to get them thinking a little about group dynamics and, unashamedly, to provide a little good humoured ice breaking. Both these exercises were remarkably successful, which pleased us since this had been the part of the three days which had caused us most anxiety. We felt that the success was in fact due to our having taken the precaution of practising a number of different exercises on a group of 'guinea pigs' and selecting the most appropriate. In the event, the sessions went well and produced a lively, relaxed and open spirit from a very early time.

The fourth of our predetermined features was the guest speaker. We were fortunate to be able to get the manager of a local office of the Department of Health and Social Security to speak to the managers about his experience of participative working in that department's radical New Model Office experiment. This down to earth detailed description of a participative process, (though in a very different organisation), by a practising manager was probably the single most influential factor in convincing the Computer Division management that participation could be a viable strategy. The provision of a prompt and efficient secretarial service to the workshop, provided by the Job Satisfaction Team's secretary was also an important element. A steady stream of minutes of sessions and amended agendas were provided as the workshop progressed. This was useful to capture the detail of what had been discussed and agreed and gave an air of professional competence to the proceedings.

Finally, we felt it was important that there should be a rapid dissemination to the whole office, in the form of a communique, of the substance of what had been discussed and agreed at the workshop. It should not, we argued, be a list of decisions taken, but a list of agreed principles to govern the future development of the office. This was in fact done at the end of the final session.

It would be tiresome to recount even the substance of all the things that the managers debated at the workshop. Our main concern was with the issue of participation and whether we could obtain some kind of agreement and commitment to undertake a project in Computer Division on the basis of our report. This was not easily accomplishc d. Our recommended approach to the organisational problems came under severe scrutiny against a background of increasing concern with the practical issues of how any group machinery might work, the time required, the identification of issues and the impact on traditional managerial authority and accountability (which were key features of the Computer Division structure and organisation). The eventual outcome of the workshop was broad agreement on a series of principles which could govern the way they would operate in the future, a rather more cohesive group of managers and a decision to invite us to launch an exercise in participative management in their organisation.

We had set out with three main aims for the workshop:

> To achieve a better climate for team working amongst the managers.

> To provide a forum for a full and detailed discussion by the managers of the wide ranging problems facing them.

> To encourage some kind of agreement or commitment to undertake a job satisfaction project on the basis of our report.

We felt that we had achieved a fair amount of success with all three of these aims. Most important of all we had achieved the agreement of the managers to some future project work and this was communicated to the office in the report of the workshop in the following fashion:

"JOB SATISFACTION

a. Management group impressed by projects in Department of Health and Social Security.

b. The Job Satisfaction Team are invited back to Computer Division to help in developing similar management methods.

c. The Senior executives and more junior grades must be involved quite quickly.

d. Details of how we proceed will be worked out with the Job Satisfaction Team."

It was against this background that we returned to Computer Division in the following week to put the project into motion.

8 The Apprehensive Staff

On reflection, the amount of effort put into convincing the small number of officers in the senior management team about the value and benefits of what we had to offer seems disproportionate when compared with the fairly haphazard way we approached the convincing of the 300 staff and their unions that the rather vague and ill-defined concept of participation and evolution represented a worthwhile and genuine way forward. In our earlier, more euphoric moments, we had talked of "lighting the blue touch paper and retiring ...". The reality was rather different! In a series of meetings with large groups of staff, with their branch managers present, we put across the philosophy and met an astonishing variety of responses - from the ecstatic to the deeply cynical. There was, however, very little outright opposition and we obtained very nearly every individual's agreement to proceed. We did feel, however, that it was a very half-hearted endorsement from the staff at large - mainly because what we were asking them to agree to was so imprecise and uncertain, not much more than an idea, with no clearly obvious practical application.

At each of the meetings with the branches we asked the branch manager to introduce the session by giving an account of what had happened at the Worthing workshop, ending up by commenting on the agreement by the management team to move towards a more genuinely participative style of management. This we felt was a valuable start since it showed that the managers were making some fairly public commitment, in front of their own staff, to the idea of participation, however unclear the concept might be. We hoped that by presenting the issue in this way we could avoid giving the impression of something being imposed from outside and that there would be seen to be a genuine opportunity for discussion and rejection of the ideas if people felt strongly that way. In the event, we suspect that the reluctance to take a stand in front of their assembled colleagues led to quite a large number of people quietly acquiescing to what was being proposed, possibly against their better judgement or instincts.

After the managers had spoken, we then were given an opportunity to expand on the philosophy. We did this in a fairly straightforward way, linking it with such concepts as grade drift (See pages 63/4), the reservoir of untapped talent in the Civil Service, the strong demand for more participation that had emerged in the diagnosis, and the programme for development outlined in our report as an expression of their own wishes brought to light during the diagnosis. We deliberately avoided describing the detail of how it all might work since that would be a matter for them to decide for themselves. As recorded above the range of response was remarkably wide but, possibly because there was so little to get their teeth into, outright opposition was limited to one or two of the smaller areas - Resource Branch where the rather older and more conservative staff decided, as they had every right to do, that participative management was not for them, and Technical Planning where rather more subtle forces

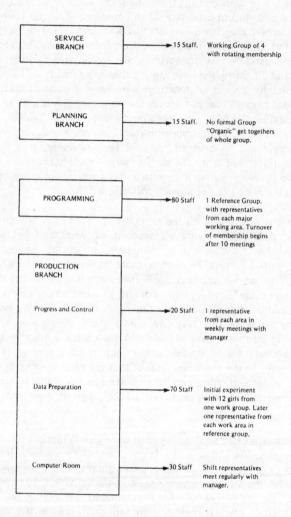

Figure 4.   Machinery of Participation.   Examples of different types of groups

concerning personalities and existing styles of management led to a rejection of our ideas. However, in both these areas, the people agreed to deal with other branches in a co-operative spirit should approaches be made to them specifically through the participative management process or machinery.

It needs to be stressed again that it would have been quite inappropriate and contrary to the underlying philosophy for a participative process to be unilaterally imposed by higher management on the staff. At the end of three weeks of meetings all branches, except Resource and Technical Planning, accepted the ideas and had set up some sort of machinery to handle what came to be called "participative management." There was no uniform type of machinery and in general the structure tended to reflect the size and characteristics of the particular branches. Some of the different types of group that emerged are shown in figure 4.

Each of these groups developed its own way of working. The differences were important since they often reflected quite substantial variations in the character, structure and size of individual branches. For instance, the two extreme cases were probably the Programming Branch reference group and the method of representation adopted by a group of specialist software staff (Operations Software), within Production Branch. In Programming Branch, the numbers involved (upwards of 70 programmers) necessitated a small representative group. This was chosen after a voluntary branch meeting (which about 50 staff attended) had decided on a method of selection. The group of five chosen at random from a list of volunteers decided at its own inaugural meeting to act in a fairly formal way - meeting regularly, publishing minutes, having a regularly rotating membership, and so on. Its function would be to receive issues raised by staff within the branch and consider them. Action might be taken by the reference group itself or by other members of the branch deputed by the reference group. The group would also act as a contact point for inter-branch activity. The relative formality and structured way of working of this group contrasted strongly with the complete informality and unstructured approach adopted by the software specialists. Here, a much smaller group (about ten people) decided that the whole staff of the section would constitute the group, that they would meet at any time to consider issues as they arose and that individual members of the group could raise issues outside the group if they felt it necessary.

These differences did not only stem from the size of the branches involved. Other small branches, for instance, Service (short term Planning Branch), decided on a relatively formal and structured approach. The nature of the work and the kind of people employed on the work also dictated the style of the response to participative management. In Operations Software the staff's view of their work was that it was providing a service, initiating new ideas and that it was interventionist. There was a clear creative element to their work and the group had been managed with a light touch accordingly. The people who seemed to gravitate to that kind of work were rather individualistic and independently minded. It was not surprising therefore that the style of representation that they adopted clearly reflected their own personalities, their view of the work they were doing, and perpetuated the existing style of management. By comparison, the formality and structure of the Programming Branch reference group reflected not only the needs of a much larger group of staff, but also flowed from the functional homogeneity of the work, the hierarchical organisation of the branch and the more formal style of management made necessary by these factors.

We now believe it to have been a flaw in our diagnosis that these differences in style and approach amongst what were both groups of programmes were not sufficiently well identified. They led to some difficulties in the early stages, particularly when relationships were being established between formal groups and informal groups. On one occasion, a meeting called by one member of an informal group led to agreements which the sponsor of the meeting thought were binding. The sponsor had not counted on the need for the representatives of more formal groups to report back and sound out opinions before formally agreeing. It also led more fundamentally to a serious questioning of the need for participative management at all. The informal, "creative" groups (Operations Software, Planning Branch and groups within Programming Branch) challenged the need to create new structures and elaborate machinery to provide opportunities for a style of management they said they were already experiencing within their branches. A variation on this argument was that, although there was a need for a more participative style of management in the division, it should be encouraged through the normal management hierarchy and that setting up alternative processes would be counter-productive. It was argued that participative management as it had emerged would hinder the ultimate aim of creating a community of workers which was free, open and responsible at all levels. Our response to these arguments was to agree that there were dangers in viewing the alternative structures as permanent features of the organisation's landscape, to stress that they were not ends in themselves and to point out that in the early stages a network of representative groups was important simply to demonstrate that something different was happening and to act as a vehicle for people to experiment with the new approach. We happily conceded that in some areas the best machinery would be no machinery at all, but that an element of trial and error in arriving at this conclusion might be no bad thing. These arguments seemed to be accepted generally, but there was a continued undercurrent of opinion to the effect that we ought to be focussing our efforts on making existing management structures work better instead of helping to establish parallel systems. In our view this rather missed the point of what we were trying to do, but we hoped this would become clearer as participative management began to develop.

Relationships with the Unions

It is probably appropriate in this description of the early stages of the project to introduce the subject of our relationships with the unions. As their attitude to what we were doing was of the utmost importance to us, we had, from the earliest days of the project, made every effort to involve the unions, represented formally by the Staff Side of the Local Office Whitley Council, in what we were doing. We talked with representatives of the unions during our first visits, and when we returned to do the diagnostic survey we asked them to carry out such tasks as vetting the interview schedule and gathering feedback from the interviewees after pilot interviews. Our diagnostic report, when written, was addressed to both management and the Staff Side. In the report we made some reference to the possible problems for unions as well as for management in what we were proposing. We had said that just as managers were being asked to take risks and delegate authority so staff side might see some of their traditional status and authority being eroded by processes aimed at creating better and more meaningful dialogue between managers and their staff.

However, despite this careful encouragement, we found their interest and involvement was mild and there was a marked lack of enthusiasm in their dealings with us at that stage. These attitudes were not helped by the publication of the report itself. It was clear from their reaction that the unions did not fully understand the ideas that we were trying to put across in the report, and any hoped for condemnation of management was largely absent from it. The report was a resounding non-event as far as the unions were concerned. This lack of understanding of what we were proposing, which we encountered with both management and staff side, underlined the need for far more preliminary discussion and preparation of the ground before a report of this kind is written. This was certainly an important piece of learning for us at this early stage in the project.

When we eventually returned to Computer Division to put into effect the participative management exercise, the unions maintained the low-key nature of their relationship with us. We met regularly with them to report progress with the various activities, but the unions wished their involvement to be of a "watchdog" kind - a passive and almost neutral stance which while not obstructive was certainly not supportive either. For instance, an early initiative from us to encourage the setting up of a joint union/management committee to oversee the progress of the project was met with indifference by the unions (and with some hostility by certain members of the management!).

It is perhaps not difficult to explain these attitudes. We were certainly something of an unknown quantity, two strangers coming to the office from outside bringing a rather unusual and nebulous message. It is true, as well, that the organisation as a whole was still a little punch-drunk from the after-effects of previous consultants' work - and here now were two more! It is, on reflection, little wonder that the unions were less than enthusiastic about our presence and what we had to offer. As mentioned above we felt that we were partly to blame for that as well.

This is probably all that needs to be said at this stage about our relationships with the unions. Later they became closer as more controversial issues were raised and we shall deal with this in due course.

9 Participation in Practice

At the end of a month a number of new groups had been established and some existing groups had been specifically nominated to handle what became known as participative management, or just 'PM'. The emphasis of this book is placed strongly on the processes of participation. We feel that it would be tedious, and very possibly rather obscure, to attempt to describe in any great detail the subject matter dealt with by the various reference groups. The topics discussed were often of a technical nature, sometimes highly specialised and difficult for the layman to comprehend properly without a deal of detailed explanation. Topics ranged widely and included such things as the design and introduction of new documentation, the devising and publishing of verification procedures, inter branch communication, divisional policy on the handling of modifications, program and system identification names, tests documentation, the implications for various parts of the division of using new programming techniques .... the list is long and subjects varied. On some of these issues only discussion took place, on others decisions were taken, on others again opinions were expressed and the matter referred to more senior managers for decision.

Working in groups was not new to many of the people who became involved in the "participative management" exercise. The working party or task group set up by management was a normal feature of working life in the office and many staff had experience of involvement in them. What was new in the participative management exercise, however, was the self-directedness of each group and the open ended nature of the tasks the groups were setting themselves. This put some strain on early meetings until the groups became familiar with the novel way of working. For instance, the Programming Branch Reference Group took all of one day at its first meeting to decide on its structure, methods of working and reporting back procedures. By the end of its seventh meeting it was carrying through a fourteen or fifteen point agenda in under two hours in a professional and efficient manner. This learning also showed itself in the voluntary self-discipline which most groups displayed in limiting the time spent on participative management meetings and activities. One group set up to look at a major cross-divisional issue had two fairly inconclusive and unstructured meetings before producing clearly defined terms of reference laying down rules for the membership of the group, the frequency of meetings, methods of investigation, and aims and objectives for their work. Another group made it clear that since their time was at a premium they could not attend meetings involving other groups unless the matter for discussion was clearly defined on paper beforehand, and they had a point of view to put. Yet another group decided, with the agreement of their branch manager, to limit their individual involvement in any formal activities connected with participative management to a maximum of one day a week. These voluntary acts of self-discipline reinforced the arguments that we had put to managers that, given responsibility, their staff would act responsibly and with commonsense.

Although there were some similarities in the behaviour of the various groups, other aspects of their working revealed quite different patterns of evolution. For instance the branch meeting which set up the Programming Branch Reference Group decided initially that it should not be a decision making body, but more a co-ordinator of activity elsewhere in the branch. In the event, the issues brought to the group were generally of a kind which did not lend themselves to this kind of treatment and the group tended to handle the matters themselves. This meant that there was not a such broadening out of participative activity within this key branch as we had originally hoped, and that the regular turnover of the Reference Group members became in the early days the main instrument for spreading participation throughout the branch. This naturally gave ammunition to those in the branch who were opposed to the way in which participative management was being handled, and who supported the view that the normal structure of management should be the proper vehicle for it. However, the response from others in the branch to a paper giving an airing to this view was surprisingly supportive of the reference group concept.

What became clear fairly early on in the activity was that the group machinery which had been newly established would need to be adaptable. A case in point was the machinery set up by the computer operators. They were operating a two-shift system so that some formality was necessary to co-ordinate views from staff on both shifts. Initially, each shift had a committee which sent a representative to a co-ordinating committee. But one shift felt this was unnecessarily formal and decided to eliminate their shift committee and nominate one representative to the co-ordinating committee only. In another part of Production Branch the trend towards informality was reversed when one group of staff who had decided on a relatively informal method of working in the beginning found that this was not meeting their needs and that a more formal structure was necessary.

Another initiative suggested that there should be "automatic interaction" between the Programming Reference Group and normal internal branch meetings. The Reference Group was "not the be all and end all" of participation. The only chance of success it was argued, was through personal involvement which was not easily achieved through the Reference Group but could be possible through some linking up of the normal internal branch meetings which everyone attended, and the Reference Group of five staff representatives. One of the Reference Group members (who was also a union representative) wrote a short paper spelling out this philosophy, and over the last year or so this linking has in fact taken place. It has been an important feature accompanying the development of a new organisational structure which is described in the next chapter. Though the Reference Group concept remains in being it is now important for its potential rather than for its actual performance. The main decision making forums of the two new major areas of the division are now open to any staff at any level. Junior staff may propose and speak to any item on the agenda providing that it has been submitted in good time. The previously highly formalised minutes are now written in christian name terms.

One particularly difficult category of problems dealt with by the machinery was that which concerned more than one branch. These issues tended to have a good deal of emotive content and generally appeared to be more important - though it is questionable whether they were - than the mundane intra branch issues. They often involved relationships between branches, the question of how particular responsibilities for work should be transferred from one group to another, or even more basic matters. The range was enormous. For instance one matter dealt with arose because the shift computer operators objected to the specialist software programmes, who were their seniors, using their rest room facilities to cook bacon and eggs. In contrast, another group looked at the whole question of the organisational structure of the Division and this is decribed in detail in Chapter 10.

The one area of the office which fell outside this categorisation was Data Preparation, the fourth stage of our original development programme. This section of seventy girls presented particular problems to us in the context of a move towards participative management. During our diagnostic interviews and brain-stormimg sessions the particular flavour of the work in Data Preparation came over strongly to us and is described in Chapter 3.

On the surface the situation in Data Preparation did not look particularly hopeful. However we had detected some important signs during our diagnostic study that suggested a potentially productive way forward. The problem was to get some meaningful participation taking place in such an area. We decided that, as a first step, the experimental group should be established, (the only real "experiment" we did). The purpose of the group would be to prove, not only to managers and unions, but also to the girls themselves, that participation was a meaningful concept in a data preparation area and that good practical results could emerge from it.

We agreed with the Production Branch manager and his Data Preparation manager that the best approach would be to select, not a group of representatives, but one particular working group of twelve girls. This idea was put to a lively meeting of all 70 data preparation girls who agreed with the approach and who chose from amongst their number one group to act as willing guinea-pigs.

The girls chose to examine the issue of the way in which errors in their punching were recorded. They held a series of meetings over a period of two months and designed and conducted an experiment in anonymous verification of their work which demonstrated quite clearly the ineffectiveness of their existing system of recording errors at verification. They eventually reported that the existing system neither helped the girls nor the managers to know what the real error rates were.

The experiment itself was, we considered, a considerable success. The outcome was that the anonymous system of verification the girls recommended was introduced throughout the Data Preparation area and a debate in management was begun around the whole question of error rates, the definition of errors and quality control. Most importantly the girls had demonstrated that they were capable of making a positive contribution.

As a result of this experiment, the management and unions, agreed that further activities towards developing a participative style of management in Data Preparation should be made. The idea was again discussed at an open meeting of all the girls in the area, and it was decided to set up a group comprising one representative from each of the working groups within the data preparation area, plus one representative from their supervisors. This group would meet regularly to discuss and make proposals on issues brought to it, both by the data preparation staff and by management.

When we left the office this development had not been an unqualified success. The girls were unsure of their role and the limits of their power; the Data Preparation manager, anxious to keep in touch with what was going on, attended part of each meeting and tended, unintentionally, to dominate proceedings and to inhibit the kind of free discussion that was essential. The issues brought to the group tended to be peripheral and not of direct concern to the work. Union anxieties about the possible undermining of their representative role in the data preparation area by participative management were also communicated to the group who, inexperienced and unsure in an unfamiliar, committee-like role, found themselves in a difficult and uncomfortable position. However the Staff Development Branch was attempting to identify these difficulties and to resolve some of the uncertainties that were worrying the members of the group.

The Third Parties

This mention of Staff Development Branch brings up an interesting aspect of the work in Computer Division. This was the use of one group of middle managers, the four training assistants, as "third parties" to assist the group processes of participation. This innovation has already been mentioned as part of our proposed programme of development work (second stage) described in Chapter 5. We felt that help from people within the organisation could be valuable for a variety of other reasons. It would immediately give the client organisation some early ownership of what was going on if some of their own staff were seen to be helping with the process. It would also relieve us from the immediate day to day oversight of project activity which, because of the very broad front on which we were operating, would have swamped us and prevented our considering the broader issues at stake. It would also involve from a very early stage the people who would have to carry on the work when we left so that experience and commitment could be built up over a reasonable period. It would inject a good deal of local knowledge, experience and expertise into the project at an early stage; and, finally, it would give meaning and impetus to that part of our original recommendation which suggested a more outgoing and interventionist role for the Staff Development Branch. We were significantly helped by the fact that the manager of the branch and his staff were generally young, sympathetic to what we were trying to accomplish and eager to assist.

The third parties were chosen because of the positions they held in the organisation and not for any particular aptitudes for the work, and we now recognise that we asked a great deal of them in the early days. They were asked to sit in on meetings with not a great deal of understanding of what they were supposed to be doing and the way they adapted to this uncertainty and developed a particular role and a distinctive style of their own speaks volumes for their flexibility and intuitive understanding of what we were about.

It became clear very early on in the project that the third party role in Computer Division would be significantly different from that in other projects we had knowledge of. Generally, the staff were a good deal more sophisticated than other groups we had worked with and, with the exception of the Data Preparation group, were familiar with and relatively at ease with group working. Working parties and task groups set up by management were already part of the working life of the office and staff, on the whole, needed little help with the processes of working in groups. The open-ended and self-directed nature of the groups that the staff set up for themselves did present some difficulties and the third parties needed to intervene on occasions to keep groups heading in the right direction. The role of the third party however did begin to change as they found that their own particular specialism - in training, career development or documentation standards - began to be called upon by the groups they were attending. In this way they began to operate less as observers and more as participant members of the various groups. This development, of course, began to enhance the role of their branch as they became more involved in issues arising throughout the Division.

This involvement was patchy and depended to some degree on the individual third party's degree of commitment and interest. This also varied with individuals and with time, but in general the involvement of the Staff Development Branch strengthened as time passed.

It was important that this should be so since the role of the branch as "guardians of the process" or "attenders of the flame" would be critical as we began to withdraw. It was clear that our position as outsiders gave us some degree of credibility as impartial observers and that when we left the internal consultants could never be seen as completely neutral. However, we felt that their early involvement and observed commitment to the work might compensate to some degree.

In assessing what their role should be when we left we came to the conclusion that they could do most of the practical day to day things that we did, but that as internal consultants they would not be able to be effective in one critical area. This was the "political" task of keeping the project activity politically neutral ie preventing it from becoming either a platform for staff agitation on the one hand or managerial authoritarianism on the other. To some extent we hoped that the creation of a sub-committee of the Local Office Whitley Council, on which management and union representatives could discuss issues arising from the participative management exercise on an equal footing, would help meet this need. It would also be the group to whom the third parties would be required to be accountable.

The role of the third parties in the delicate stage of our handing over project ownership to the office and withdrawal was particularly important. We agreed with them and the management group that they would continue to act in the semi-process consultant, semi-specialist/expert role, and that their branch manager would act as the link with senior management (he was a member of the senior management team) and with the unions. Regular separate progress meetings with senior managers and the unions were held and the Staff Development Branch has presided over the gradual absorption of the participative management process into the normal day to day running of the office.

The Managers and the Unions

The success of the 'alternative' group decision-making machinery as a vehicle for achieving attitudinal change amongst subordinates seeking to reduce their dependency, and managers, needing to question their 'automatic prerogative' to make unilateral decisions, depended to a large degree on the attitudes and actions of the most senior managers. They, by the very nature of the exercise, were being asked to give up some of the power and influence they wielded within the organisation, whilst at the same time retaining responsibility for the end results and outputs. The extent to which different managers were prepared to do this varied considerably, as did the degree of pain and anxiety the process caused them. Some managers seemed to take to it naturally and easily, others experienced, quite sharply, the ambiguity and uncertainty of a new and untried process which challenged their basic assumptions about managers rights and responsibilities - as one manager said to us "I've put my head in a noose. . ."

This anxiety was apparent in the early hesitation to undertake the project and in the imposition of the constraint that on no account should the new organisational structure be changed. The managers, quite understandably, were frightened of the possible consequences. In a very real sense they had put their careers at risk.

We were, therefore, very encouraged in the very early days of the project that when managers were putting across to their staff their views of what participative management was, they defended it strongly against some fairly critical questioning. But after the initial flush of enthusiasm for the bright new idea we noted increasing uncertainty amongst some managers. This was caused mainly by the failure of some of the groups that the staff had set up to communicate with the managers about what subjects were being debated and how they were operating. This had a particularly unsettling effect in the bigger branches (Programming and Production) where numbers alone meant that the managers were necessarily more distant from the lower levels of their staff than in the small branches. Both managers involved here took their own steps to find out what was going on, initiating meetings with the Reference Groups, obtaining copies of group minutes and setting up meetings with representatives from a variety of groups. The role of the consultant is worth touching on here. We could not assume the anxiety of the managers for them. We helped when we could by talking through the problems with them, counselling a "wait and see" (or "grin and bear it") policy and seeking to develop the essential feelings of trust in the innate responsibility and good sense of their staff.

Interestingly from our point of view, the first major issue to arise in one branch was in the nature of a challenge, (albeit a fairly minor one), to the authority of the branch manager. It consisted of a proposal to abolish the lunch-time cover for one aspect of production work, a policy known to be contrary to the wishes of the manager. The manager's first reaction was to say "nothing doing" but he was persuaded to see what happened when the proposal was put, as it had to be, to the representative groups of other branches who might need to use the lunch-time cover facility. In the event, every other group agreed that no formal lunch-time cover was needed and the manager was persuaded to accept what he still saw as a deterioration in the service his branch was offering, on an experimental basis. (The new system has subsequently worked smoothly). A concession by the manager on this issue was probably helped by discussion with a consultant and, we are sure, materially altered the climate towards participative management in that branch.

This particular issue, whilst it was on the one hand a muted challenge to the manager personally, was on the other hand a fairly open challenge to the whole concept of participative management. This illustrates another aspect of the manager position which made their role in the early days of the exercise particularly difficult. The question of their credibility and the genuineness of their motives was something that formed a continuous undercurrent to the exercise - did management really mean what they said; were they really preparing to loosen the reins of control, even a little; would it all come to nothing when the consultants finally left the office? The consultant's role here was completely reversed. We were now saying to the staff - "who can say what the real motives are, only time and trusting relationship will tell". We found ourselves adjuring both sides to trust each other, and these us/them attitudes were a constant theme which underlay all the project activity.

These issues of trust, credibility and responsibility came to a head in the very thorny question of the effect of participation on the problem of managerial responsibility and authority. A key theme in our early arguments in favour of participative management had been that the Civil Service had experienced a high degree of "grade drift" in recent years - a phenomenon by which responsibility and decision making authority had been drawn up the hierarchy, so that decisions and responsibilities which had, in years gone by, lain with officers in one particular grade had tended to become the tasks of people higher up the organisation. A common criticism would be "I'm a senior manager now, but I used to take decisions like the ones I have to take now when I was a junior member of staff, twenty years ago!" Our argument was that grade drift was bad for morale, job satisfaction and efficiency. It actively worked against the principle of participation and should be reversed. We saw participative management as helping this reversal by relocating decision making authority at the "right" levels ie where the proper experience, detailed knowledge and ability existed. Decisions were being taken too high in the organisation so that those who were directly affected had little or no influence on the decisions and could often see flaws in what had been decided. The reversal of grade drift could be interpreted as a matter of delegation, but the establishment of group decision making machinery, with discretion to decide unilaterally what they wished to discuss, raised more serious questions of managerial authority and responsibility. In an organisation like Computer Division with its philosophy of tight functional control and accountability, the free-wheeling kind of processes that we were advocating were naturally viewed with some suspicion and scepticism. How could a manager delegate authority yet still retain responsibility; could groups receive delegated authority and how could you ensure that they acted responsibly if that authority was vested in no one person; how could branch managers remain accountable in organisational terms if they were no longer exercising authority or had responsibility? The permutations on this theme seemed almost endless and all were equally impossible to answer. Our replies were that these were all good, theoretical issues based on hypothetical situations; what we had to do was to try participation out in practice and reply to the theoretical questions with empirical answers. We tried on occasions to ask managers, (and this applied not only at branch manager level but at all levels of management), to examine the reality of their "authority", "responsibility" and "accountability" - did these concepts really have substance, or, more cynically, were we all subordinates in the Civil Service with no real responsibility and accountability whatsoever? These questions were never properly resolved and never really caused any great heart searching in practice, both of which tended to support our view that the reality of responsibility and accountability in the public sector is minimal. The argument that seemed to be accepted - it was at least very rarely challenged - was that whilst a manager might delegate authority, that act of delegation could not absolve him from the responsibility and accountability attached to the post he occupied. It also seemed to be accepted that authority could be delegated to a group on a collective basis. A variation on these arguments was the attempt to define what was a "management decision" and what was a decision appropriate for Reference Groups to take, and where did one draw the dividing line? We had advocated a policy by which decisions could be taken "at the appropriate level" in the organisation and we were constantly being asked to define what was an "appropriate level". There is of course no hard and fast definition for either of these propositions and we therefore had to continue to repeat that the "appropriate" level was where the best combination of skill, experience and ability lay to handle a particular issue, that this could not be determined *a priori* and could only be resolved empirically by examining each issue as it arose.

It was against this background that we implemented the third stage of our proposal for a programme of organisation development which involved support for the top management team.

Our aims were broadly;

> to get the managers to spell out how far they were prepared to 'loosen the reins' and to be able to perceive how far the process had developed. We wanted to give them confidence that participation was not an uncontrollable process.

> to give them ownership of the process by encouraging them to report on what was happening in their branch and what developments were likely. Evidence of tangible change would be important to them particularly in the early phase, to demonstrate that the scheme was practical.

> to derive learning from what was going on.

> to develop a cohesive and mutually supportive climate in the top management team as a whole, not only in respect of participation but as a way of improving their general decision making capacity.

> to be able to observe any changes in management style taking place.

The more structured aspects of this programme took place in the fortnightly management meetings attended by at least one of us. These always had "participative management developments" as an agenda item. Here each manager reported from his particular branch perspective, the progress of particular groups was commented upon and the whole exercise subjected to general scrutiny and discussion.

The more informal aspects took place in day to day 'chats' with individual managers. From the consultants point of view it was essential to know where each manager 'was at'. Each manager started from their existing managerial style and developed at their own pace towards more open relationships. Changes in managerial style do not happen overnight and when they are perceived they need to be reinforced. A change in management style implies a change in attitude. An attitude can be defined as a tendency to act in certain ways under certain conditions, and it is the visible behavioural act which is conclusive evidence of change, though what the managers said was also important. Thus one of the more reserved managers was happier to see participation in terms of delegation rather than recognising the clear implications for the power structure, and constantly spoke about it in 'delegation' terms. When at one Reference Group the comment was made rather jokingly that their manager "stops and chats to us on the stairs now" it was significant. We did not underestimate how difficult he might be finding such casual behaviour. We kept our day by day diary in part to enable such changes to be identified and recorded.

One final example of behavioural change will suffice. Towards the end of our time one of the senior managers asked to see us. He said that though in the early days he had had significant doubts about participation he was now convinced of its value to the extent that it might alter the future path of his career. He was questioning the whole way he had managed people in the past and was leaning towards the view that he should act as a supportive "consultant" to his staff. He cited a particular issue where he was trying to put this into practice. All sorts of doubts and questions crowded in upon him which we could understand and share but could not solve for him. It was quite apparent that the participative process was changing his patterns of behaviour to a significant degree.

Relationships with the Unions

From the very earliest days of the project, we made every effort to involve the unions, represented formally by the Staff Side of the Local Office Whitley Council, in what we were doing, and we have described the rather cool reception we received in the early days in Chapter 8.

This ambivalence was present right through until the time of the union elections when new representatives were elected and we had a partially new body of union officers to deal with. Several important threads in the work began to come together at this time. Some of the groups were beginning to discuss issues which clearly overlapped with those that unions had traditionally viewed as their own, ie accommodation and, in the Data Preparation area, the proficiencey payment scheme, were some of the early ones.

Another way in which this new interest began to show itself was in the drawing-up by the unions of a "code of practice" for reference groups. It was hoped to show that a line could be drawn to separate those issues which were legitimate for the reference groups to deal with and those which the unions wished to handle, though in fact this attempted codification was never referred to in subsequent project activity. It is interesting to note that the top management group has also established guidelines for group activities by drawing up a remarkable similar type of "code of practice". These problems put a good deal of strain on some individuals who felt dual loyalty to both union and reference group activity.

Relationships with the unions generally remained relatively superficial throughout but they certainly gradually improved and became positive rather than neutral. This lack of involvement was partly explained by constraints of time. Union officers had a job to do as well as perform their union tasks. It was only over the question of the interim review of participative management described later, in Chapter 12, that the union officers became more deeply involved in aspects of project activity.

Summing up the unions response it is clear that they viewed the process with suspicion. This was based on two main fears stemming from the following premise;

"Management only do things to get something out of it. Participative management is another 'management con' aimed at:

Short Term

i.   getting staff to do higher quality work without paying for it. If junior staff were taking more important decisions they ought to be rewarded for the extra responsibility.

Long Term

ii.   Usurping the union role, traditionally based on negotiating and bargaining with management on a collective basis. Union power is based on collectivism whereas participation allows expression to individuals. A great diversity of views from union members, would weaken the 'unity is strength, philosophy and possibly set union members against each other."

Union officers faced a real dilemma when confronted with the need to maintain the collective unity of their membership in the face of a process which offered those same members a greater individual say in the management of their organisation. These issues are touched on again in Chapter 16.

10 The Topic Orientation Group

This chapter describes the activities of the inter-branch group which was concerned with organisational structure. Inter-branch groups developed somewhat later in the project activity and whilst intra branch groups tended to deal with day to day matters, the inter-branch groups sprang up under particular stimuli to consider specific issues with wider ramifications.

The closer study of this particular group is worthwhile because it illustrates in more detail what trying to introduce a process of learning and evolution involves. It is important to emphasise that because the group was constituted sometime after the initial activity began it operated in a climate that was already showing more openness. An example of this was the debate in Programming Branch about the form of the participative machinery that had been established there. A particular group of programmers had opposed the machinery of groups from the beginning because it implied that "participation was something different from good management". They argued that managers were paid to manage and that a good manager would consult his staff anyway. Special group machinery was thus unnecessary. Consultation was what happened in their own section and in a rather self-congratulatory way they circulated a note which suggested that their form of consultative management should be copied by other areas. Some of the written comments from other programmers made in response to this initiative are given below:

> "The group have brought up a number of valid points which deserve consideration. I agree that the two main problems are communication and the inefficiency of management, I agree that these are problems which need to be overcome but how? Certainly not by studying *them* as the ideal team! They discuss problems with their middle manager. Has it never occurred to them that some junior staff find it very difficult to approach their middle managers about any problems?"

> "I agree however that there is a feeling that managers are neglecting to manage, but to assume the Reference Group is taking on a powerful role rather than the rather tedious job it actually has, is missing the point. Overall though, I think some of the criticisms are justified but, accepting the existence of the Reference Group, surely these grouses can be positively directed through the group".

> "They should have given the Reference Group more of a chance before condemning it".

> "As a statement of the group's views, there are some good points with which I would agree. As an exercise in generating bad feeling and animosity among programmers however it must be unsurpassed."

Whilst it is certain that the young staff would tend to be outspoken anyway, there appeared to have been no similar example of such a public debate having taken place before on any comparable issue. The project had caught the interest of the staff who had earlier in the diagnostic phase described themselves, (or more correctly their fellow workers), as apathetic and lethargic. There was nothing apathetic or lethargic about these responses. The staff were thinking about what was going on and feeling it worthwhile to contribute.

The Establishment of the Topic Orientation Group

(In the following account, 4 levels of staff are identified, Top, Senior, Middle and Junior).

During the early days of the project, the Senior staff had been uncertain exactly where they stood in relation to participation. They had not been involved in the top management workshop which first accepted the principle of participation, subject to agreement by the rest of the staff. They had attended the subsequent series of branch meetings with middle and junior staff where this agreement had been forthcoming but here they had been a small element among much larger numbers. They possibly felt that their position merited more weight being accorded to their views than had in fact been given. The doubts concerning the merits of participation were particularly well developed in the Planning Branch where the top manager had a series of informal meetings with his seniors attempting to establish with them exactly what participation meant.

The matter of senior manager involvement came to a head quite suddenly and is an illustration of the speed with which a major issue can suddenly become a matter of action after apparently lying dormant. It also illustrates the vested interest which motivates much of the internal activity in organisations and helps create the political climate in which an interventionist operates. (see Chapter 13).

A routine meeting had been arranged between six senior managers in the programming area and a consultant to discuss the seniors' involvement in participation. This meeting was transformed overnight by the senior planners into a meeting of all senior managers in the operational area. The senior planners had earlier circulated a paper which sought to question the whole concept of participation. It quickly became clear that the planners were not going to get support for this line from their colleagues in other branches who said that the discussion was academic, for in their areas there was no possibility of turning the clock back. The process of participation was already too well established.

One senior planner then suggested that perhaps the seniors could use participation "at our level for our own ends" and suddenly proposed that the group should turn its attention to considering the structure of the organisation!

A comment followed that "six or seven of the most experienced people in the organisation" (a group which would clearly include the speaker), could quickly design a better organisation. This produced a reaction from those present who were more committed to participation, (or if not committed, who managed large numbers of participating staff), who said that this elitist approach was quite out of line with the philosophy of participation. A later remark was that some of the attitudes being displayed might indicate that the participative process was more like "fascism than maoism". A more moderate tone was introduced and agreement was eventually reached that a group of middle and junior staff with senior involvement should be formed to examine the structure of the organisation and make proposals for any changes thought necessary. The senior planner who had been responsible for initiating the meeting was nominated as one of the senior representatives to sit on the group.

Thus the Topic Orientation Group, irreverently known as "Poo Group" (Project Orientated Organisation), came into being with representatives being nominated by each of the various areas involved. Our dominant strategy was simply to get the parties, all with their particular interests, to consider in an atmosphere of mutual respect what they had learned about the operation of the organisation since its inception two years earlier, and see if any improvement could be made. Any adaption to the existing structure thought necessary would only be feasible if it was compatible with all the interests represented. If no agreement could be reached than at least each party would be better able to understand the reasons for any obdurate or critical stance adopted by another interest. It was hoped that at least this might reduce some of the hostility which was apparent in the organisation between various parties with competing interests.

The main purpose of the Topic Orientation Group was, as its name suggests, to consider the possibility of modifying the structure of Computer Division from one which was strongly functional in character (with staff being organised by their function eg programmers, analysts, operators) towards one in which staff were organised by reference to the work topic they dealt with (eg broadly Census, Statistics and Social Survey). The broad structural differences involved can be seen by comparing Figures 1 and 5. From a job satisfaction point of view the topic oriented alternative offered some advantages with improved scope for involvement by programmers and analysts in a wider range of professional tasks, and identification with a recognisable block of work and the customers for whom it was done. The Topic Orientation Group comprised about twelve people consisting of representatives from Planning, Service, Programming and Production Branch. One of the authors and an internal third party, who acted as facilitator and secretary, also attended meetings. Some of the particular interests of the parties who sat around the table are worth identifying:

Senior Planners They were primarily responsible for the group's existence. They were the most experienced ADP staff but had little managerial responsibility, for, as systems analysts, their subordinates operated as professional equals. (In fact to establish some measure of status distinction one evening after the junior planners had gone home their seniors moved all their desks to one end of the room). A main interest was that in the existing functional organisation their control was limited to planning work. Any delays in programming or production were outside their influence though they faced outwards to the customer and received brickbats about delayed work. In a topic oriented structure it was likely that they, as the most experienced staff would become project leaders with significant managerial control across all operational areas.

Junior and Middle Planners These were in general ex-programmers who were developing experience as analysts. They were seen in the organisation as an elite, and were highly satisfied with their jobs. They foresaw that with the development of project teams in a topic oriented organisation they were likely to have to share their analyst function and take on some programming work which was disagreeable to them.

Junior and Middle grades of Service Branch (Short Term Planning) These again had originally been seen as a rather elitist branch but in fact much of the ad hoc work they were involved in tended to be routine and this had caused dissatisfaction. However the branch was small and had a strong sense of identity. The key to this identity lay in three young ladies of strong character and considerable ADP experience. The branch had recently been subjected to an external manpower audit and it was clear that it was likely to be disbanded. The staff involved gradually came to accept this but were concerned that some of their functions should remain, even if carried out by another branch. Most importantly they were concerned that they could disband with dignity and a topic oriented structure offered this possibility.

Junior Programmers The programmers were by far the largest group of professional ADP specialists and had found the stricter definition of task and narrower terms of reference introduced in the functional structure not much to their liking. Many of them were interested in getting a broader range of duties, including analysts tasks, re-establishing links back to the customers and forwards to the computer in "running their own jobs".

Production The production area did not have too high a regard for programmers abilities. When a "run" broke down they saw it as due to slackness and inefficiency in Programming Branch. They generally supported the existing functional structure and were keen to maintain an independent existence.

These are just a few of the tensions present at the outset of the Topic Orientation Group meeting. As the group progressed other pressures were generated by top management who were anxious to find out what was going on; personality differences between individuals emerged and subsided; coalitions between interests were forged and disbanded according to the progress of the discussions. The level of frustration and tension generally remained high for all concerned throughout the period of the group's discussions. Some themes

71

concerning the processes of group meetings can usefully be drawn out from our experience with this group.

Nature of the Group's Discussions

Groups can operate in various ways. For instance one man can run the meeting as chairman largely controlling discussion or the meeting can operate as a committee. It is perhaps possible to postulate four types of group meetings:

Types of Group Power structures

a.   Chairman - here the sanction lies with one person.

b.   Committee - here the sanction lies with the majority.

c.   Multi-professional - here the sanction lies with each in his role of expert.

d.   Power Blocs - here the sanction lies with any power group.

The Topic Orientation Group operated generally on the lines of the power bloc model though as agreement was reached the group became more cohesive and faced outwards to the organisation as a united committee.

The early meetings of the group were marked by a degree of confusion. As Figure 2 indicates, it appears that ADP personnel have a fairly high need to operate in an unambiguous environment. Here there was considerable ambiguity. They were not sure whether or not they had the right to be actually considering the future of the organisational structure at the behest of senior managers - *not* top managers. They were not sure that it was possible, given the different interests present, the likely attitudes of which they had more than an inkling, to reach agreement. They were doubtful whether anything would come of it for there was a measure of disbelief that top management would let them influence anything. Comments were made which reflected a desire to return to the traditional order of things. These and other reservations combined during the course of the group's meetings to produce moves to establish more certainty.

The Group in Disarray

When the first meetings took place to discuss the sort of organisation that might emerge discussion was dominated by a senior planner. He presented a description of the form of organisation that he favoured, at the same time remarking "I am all for this form of participation but not in the actual decision making".

A few days later a secret gathering of the junior planners was held without the knowledge of their senior colleagues. Comments were made that "the senior managers should not have produced a blue print for us to comment on" and that "terms of reference were needed". There was also hints that the senior staff had dominated the last meeting. The probable reason for this reaction was that after the recent meeting the junior planners had become sharply aware of the difference between their interests in keeping their elitist analyst position and their senior colleagues who wanted to extend their control. The message was wrapped up in a lot of other noise about the difficulty of finding the time to attend participative meetings and whether it was all worthwhile anyway. It was also suggested the Production Branch (known as likely to oppose any change in structure), should be represented. The junior planners agreed to put these views to the full group. At the next meeting the senior level were asked to withdraw, it was agreed that Production Branch should be invited and terms of reference and a timetable for action were drawn up.

Elements of the Group in Flight

The Topic Orientation Group then settled down to some serious work. The advantages and disadvantages of the existing organisation were set out and a number of papers produced which suggested various ways in which the organisation could be changed or adapted. During this period all the papers, together with the minutes, were given wide circulation in the division and these were backed up by the personal discussions conducted by the representatives in their various areas. Written comments were also invited and submitted on specific issues by anyone who wished to contribute. (Even so this fairly widespread democratic process was criticised as not giving sufficient information; a cardinal lesson to be drawn is that information and participation generate demands for yet more information. Compared with the earlier experience of introducing organisational change when the Division was originally set up the information was now truly abundant!).

73

As the progress advanced the junior planners again became increasingly uneasy. They mentioned that they had doubts about the terms of reference, (which they had largely drawn up themselves), they felt they were being manipulated, (though not by the external interventionist they hurriedly added), and reiterated that they did not think top management would let anything be done. With Production Branch now in the group, Service Branch and Programming Branch representatives tended to form a coalition change against Planning and Production. Production adopted a low profile which became lower as time went on with comments normally restricted to heavy sighs. Egan [1] has described how individuals can engage in flight behaviour in groups as follows:

A Flight Behaviour Model

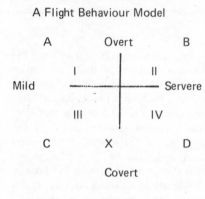

1.   Point A - Mild overt behaviour eg "We don't have to do it"

2.   Point B - Severe overt behaviour eg Open Flight

3.   Point C - Mild covert behaviour eg Passing joke breaks tension.

4.   Point D - Severe covert behaviour eg Agressive and disruptive.

Production representatives began and remained non-committed and for the most part silent at point X. They were not interested in change and saw that because of the separate nature of their position in the organisation they could probably remain untouched by any changes. Programming representatives were anyway too busy wrestling with Planning to devote energy to a secondary interest of extending their activities to the computer room. However the junior planners began to engage in more serious and overt flight behaviour as Service Branch and the programmers increasingly bickered with them. After some experience of this coupled with less than active support from Production Branch the attendance of the planners at meetings began to fall off though one particular representative remained throughout, often working in his own time. He played a major part in shaping the future course of events. Had he given up it would have been extremely difficult, given the power bloc nature of group deliberations, to have continued with the group. As it was he had to face the rest of his branch and justify his position and involvement to them, including the two whose attendance had become intermittent. (The exact nature of this relationship is not clear though it is perhaps relevant that this particular person had been made twice redundant earlier in his career in commercial ADP organisations following "re-organisation". It is possible that his position was somewhat uncomfortable but nevertheless he persevered).

A most interesting feature was that the papers presented by the two main sides, Programming and Planning really had very little between them. What was holding back agreement seemed to be largely personal considerations. Throughout the process members of the group had informal conversations with the consultant. For instance the Planning Branch representatives would freely admit their interest in maintaining their elitist position at group meetings but privately said it was "personality problems in the group" which were preventing a solution. On another occasion it was privately suggested that planners were "failing to grasp the conceptual structure and being worried about personal factors". It was only slowly that they began to be more constructive. When they began to put aside hostility, possibly under pressure to conform with the time-scale earlier established, agreement was reached. Agreement inevitably represented a compromise between the different interests, but it was acceptable to all of them. At this stage the group, committed to their decision, began to operate more as a united committee. The content of the agreement was restricted to broad aspects rather than details and proposed that the organisation could and should evolve towards a topically oriented structure.

The Top Managerial Attitude

The top managers, themselves still somewhat confused themselves about the philosophy of participation, re-acted in various ways to the progress of the Topic Orientation Group. At first they seemed content to let the discussion proceed. One manager who kept his ear very much to the ground remarked with a smile early on "I gather they feel they have bitten off more than they can chew". The advent of any move towards a topic structure was obviously going to have an effect on the distribution of top managerial jobs. In addition, any change in organisational structure within specified levels of staff clearly had a manipulative potential for outflanking any staff cuts imposed by the manpower auditors. There were also pressures from customers, particularly on the Head of Division, for more direct influence on the work. These users were known to favour a move to some form of project orientation in the processing of their work as a means of recovering some of their previous influence on events in the ADP field.

A major role for us was to ensure that these political pressures from outside the group did not interfere with its progress. In spite of the difficulties within the group a gradual confidence developed that they were going to be able to have significant influence. This changing attitude was quickly communicated and recognised by some of the top management. Suggestions began to be made by some of them that possibly the relatively junior staff involved - particularly in the light of the departure of the senior staff from the group - were unlikely to have sufficient experience to consider the implications of a topic structure in depth. Other comments related to the fact that top managers ought to be given more information about what was going on. (As a response to this both the Head of Division and his deputy met the group on successive days to receive some feedback on progress. Following this meeting one of them remarked he was more worried than before - group members were becoming 'dogmatic' and "had the bit between their teeth''. He had just been told by one member of the group that junior staff's views should be given equal weight with those of senior staff). In contrast one top manager was content to allow the group to come up with specific proposals which, if they were accepted as representing a majority view in the Division, should be implemented. Another supported leaving the group alone to "allow the junior staff view to be heard''. The key features of these attitudes were uncertainty as to what was going on, unhappiness about their lack of control and doubts about the ability of the junior staff. There was a degree of mistrust about the whole process. One manager put it neatly "it is an exact reversal - rather than junior staff getting concerned about what top managers are up to and seeking to find out what is going on, it is the top managers who are doing the wondering''.

Following the production of the written proposals by the Topic Orientation Group there was a problem of how to bring senior staff back into the process. Apart from comments they had submitted to the group there had been little direct involvement after they left. The original aim had been to have a multi-grade group presenting proposals for top management consideration. With the disappearance of the seniors from the group it had now become necessary to build in a further process to integrate the senior views. To reach a participative decision it would be necessary to somehow bring together the four elements (junior, middle, senior and top management) into a consensus.

The first step undertaken by the Topic Orientation Group was to circulate their final paper widely throughout the office and to arrange half-day talk-ins, separately, for each of the elements. At these meetings a panel from the Topic Orientation Group answered queries and clarified their arguments. At the second talk-in with the senior level staff it became clear that there was no hope of unanimous support for the juniors' proposal. Consequently we were asked to set up a meeting of all seniors involved to discuss the implications of this and a smaller representative group of seniors was established. The coalition in this group tended to be different from the junior group. Here the planners and programmers generally were in harmony. Only production representatives argued strongly against the recommendations, but as their branch was not included in the proposal they did not press their opposition. The main outcome from the discussions in the senior group was a council of caution emphasizing that any changes should build on existing developments and be over an extended period. They however supported the main argument of the junior group in that they agreed that there should be a gradual development towards a topically oriented pattern of organisation. The seniors reached this decision with surprising speed considering the early significant differences within the group. There was undoubtedly an anxiety to avoid too much open disagreement and to demonstrate that they, too, were able to reach an orderly concensus.

These discussions took place over a period of six months. At the end of that time it was clear that there was widespread support for organisational change. The Top management group agreed that the issue was of such importance that a workshop should be arranged where representatives of all groups should sit down together to consider the evidence

NOTES

[1] G Egan, 'Encounter', Brooks Cole, 1970.

11 The Participative Workshop

A programme for the workshop was devised which was flexible but which covered the two main emerging themes;

evaluation of participative management

decisions about topic orientation

The flexibility built into the structure was crucial. Some structure was necessary to provide a framework for thought and administration, but the facility to adapt or alter the timetable was essential and, in the event, well used.

The workshop was held at the Civil Service College at Sunningdale over a three day period. The first session was scheduled as "management evaluation of participative management". Here the top managers considered their own performance as a group since participation began and what were their "Hopes, Fears and Expectations" of the following three days. In attempting to assess the performance of the team over the previous nine months, the members discussed the concept of a team, whether it was consistent with the need for each branch manager to represent the views and opinions of his staff and whether the emphasis on the management team as a decision making body discouraged lower level small group decision making. At this point, some of the comments which the managers themselves had made over the previous nine months were fed back to them. Such comments as:

"I feel that we have not operated well as a team because the individual managers have been busy defending or defining their branch boundaries."

"Conflicts between the branch heads have caused some ill-feeling."

"Some differences in opinion or approach have gone on too long underlying discussions between managers where it would have been better to bring the differences to the surface and resolve them."

There was still a feeling that even the present discussions were not as full and frank as they might be; that problems were not isolated or defined properly, and that there was still too much inconclusive discussion. Some felt that there was still a tendency at times for branch managers to defend their own branch and not always to show a united front. This, they said, could sometimes produce a tendency to snipe at common decisions, and the differences between members of the top management group were quickly perceived and mirrored at lower levels. The very fact that the top managers were able to talk so frankly to each other about these issues in contrast to the situation at the earlier workshop was immensely encouraging.

Against this background the team turned to examine their "Hopes, Fears and Expectations" about the following 2½ days. The chief fears were;

that after 2½ days of inconclusive discussion no decisions would be reached.

that the the meeting with the topic structure groups on the following day the managers would appear in complete disarray.

The chief hopes were

that conclusions would be reached about a topic structure and the future of participative management.

that in meeting with the topic structure groups, the top managers would appear objective and sympathetic and would have an ordered approach to these sessions.

The chief expectations were;

that some kind of guidelines on both issues would be reached

that all or some of the people coming would go away dissatisfied.

The exposure of their expressed fear of inconclusive debate was valuable and was used skilfully by several of the managers during the following sessions.

For the rest of the first day the top management team considered topic orientation itself. It is important to emphasis that they did not attempt to pre-empt any decision which might result from the joint meeting arranged for the following day. This discussion was the first occasion the top management group had formally considered the proposal. The discussion centred on the concept of a topic oriented organisation and how it would affect the division. What were the reasons for introducing a topic organisation and what were likely to be the problems? What were the various forms it could take? Throughout this day of discussion there was an air of tension among the management group about the next days events. A group of a dozen well informed staff were going to sit down with the top management team to discuss the future form of the organisation. Would the credibility of the top management team suffer as a result of this contact or might the whole day become a shambles of mutual recrimination?

The agenda for the second day had been devised with our assistance and included a morning of syndicate discussions. Each syndicate was designed to include junior, middle, senior and top management. The purpose of this was two-fold. First to break the ice between the arriving staff and the top managers and secondly to focus discussion on various important points of organisational

79

change which had not been fully aired in earlier discussion. The syndicate session was followed by a verbal report from each of the elements, junior, senior and top management as to how they saw the organisation needing to develop.

The use of the syndicates as a team building and integrating process was successful. Common problems were talked through to give some kind of continuity, and to establish some base-line for the future.

The whole morning, including the report-back session, was spent on information gathering. This helped establish some important common ground ie that there existed general agreement that topic orientation was the right direction for the division to move in; that the speed of advance should be slow, and gradual evolution the key-note; and that there was a need for an early decision.

After lunch the first hour was again very constructive and the group appeared to be quickly coming to a decision. Everyone in the group was invited to speak and there was no domination of the group by any one personal interest. Then it suddenly began to go wrong as discussion disgressed and regressed. Peripheral matters were raised and the whole central theme of considering the general issue of organisational change became lost. We warned the group that they appeared to be going backwards but it got worse. One of the representatives a planner, (the one largely responsible for initiating the original group), made, on the spur of the moment, what seemed to be a complete reversal of his position and the arguments presented by the group to which he had contributed. Throughout this unreal period the atmosphere remained harmonious.

After over an hour of this - and with no specific chairman it was likely to go on - tea arrived just as there were signs that the group was returning to the central theme. The newly established train of thought of the group was broken for with one accord the membership rose from their seats and encircled the trolley. General conversation broke out.

This was a serious situation. The visiting group were due to leave in less than an hour and there was no agreement, though it was clear all the ingredients for it were present. Getting the group together in an atmosphere divorced from day to day interruptions was by no means easy. Six months of work by the group was at risk! At this point one of us called the meeting to order, drew attention to the situation and asked them to continue their discussions. (Interestingly, we later learned that the situation was viewed very differently by some of the managers who felt that things were very much more in control than we did. Our attempt to pull things back on the rails was seen by some to be a hinderance rather than a help!) Within a short space of time a specific proposal by the Head of Division to appoint two managers to head particular project areas rather than functional areas was made, commented upon and agreed by all present. A target date was also agreed and it was affirmed that all aspects of moving towards the new order would have to be preceded by extensive discussions with those involved.

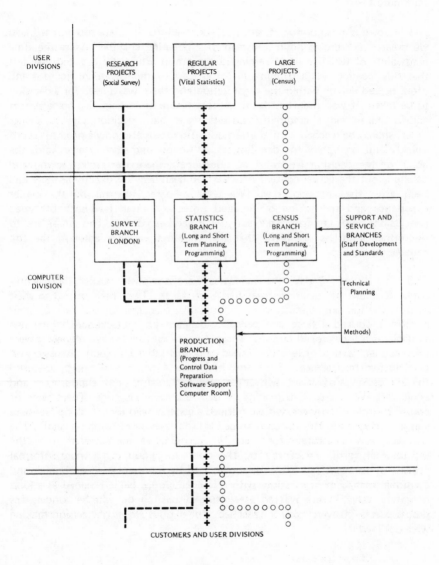

USER DIVISIONS

RESEARCH PROJECTS (Social Survey)

REGULAR PROJECTS (Vital Statistics)

LARGE PROJECTS (Census)

COMPUTER DIVISION

SURVEY BRANCH (LONDON)

STATISTICS BRANCH (Long and Short Term Planning, Programming)

CENSUS BRANCH (Long and Short Term Planning, Programming)

SUPPORT AND SERVICE BRANCHES (Staff Development and Standards

Technical Planning

PRODUCTION BRANCH (Progress and Control Data Preparation Software Support Computer Room)

Methods)

CUSTOMERS AND USER DIVISIONS

Fig 3.   Computer Division as at November 1976

A note setting out these decisions was circulated throughout the office on the following day. Figure 5 shows how the organisation appeared some months later (cf Figure 1).

The obvious question for us here was "Did we force the pace too much?" Had we created a "forcing house" instead of a debating chamber? Were the time constraints of which we had reminded the group artificially induced? We felt that this meeting was a culmination of at least six months, long, rigorous and often heated debate within the organisation and there was a need for a decision to be taken. It was important for us, for the future of participative management and for the managers' credibility and self image that a decision, one way or the other, should be reached on that afternoon. There was also now a need to record quickly and accurately the decision taken. Almost immediately afterwards the detail of the decision began to be questioned; there was back-tracking and debate about the actual content of what had been decided, exactly as there had been after the first workshop. We were prepared for this by the earlier experience and the taking of detailed notes and rapid feed-back of typed conclusions helped to establish exactly what had been decided and put an end to the rather pointless argument that then began to emerge amongst the top management group.

On the following day, the managers were obviously relaxed, and gently euphoric about the decisions that had been taken. They then turned to their own evaluation and discussion of participative management and one of their number produced a large and complex **diagram** on a blackboard which was valuable as a focus for discussion. There is no doubt that the top managers were now content and a little self-satisfied and this led to a good discussion on participative management. They now had some experience of the process and the discussion was laced with examples and reality, not supposition and conjecture. We were all beginning to talk the same language. There were of course still big differences and we noticed a general need for "stroking" ie there was a need amongst the managers to be told that they were "doing it right". The managers saw a natural progression in participative management from the institutional form represented by the reference groups to a more informal process of participation within branches and by representation on branch and divisional management meetings with reference groups being retained as a kind of safety valve. There was an interesting discussion on whether under this process decisions were taken or reached. The various stages of decision making were outlined ie

   i.   data collection

   ii.   discussion and analysis of the data

   iii.   forming proposals

   iv.   taking decisions

v.   implementation

vi.   evaluation.

It seemed that in the topic structure groups we had seen stages i to iv come under the participative management umbrella with v and vi still remaining to be tackled. For us, the three day workshop was probably the high spot of the whole project. We had seen how a major organisational change had been discussed throughout the organisation and had now been generally agreed - an organisation costing £150,000 in consultants time and fees was now being redesigned by the concerted efforts of interested parties at all levels within the office. Major changes had now been made, and seen to be made, through the processes of direct participation. Things would never be quite the same again. It was clear that taking the one decision on topic structure made necessary a lot of other changes. For instance, decisions on career development, training, accommodation, new working relationships and a whole range of technical issues involving the user divisions and other interested outsiders all remained to be tackled. But the decision reached at the workshop was a significant turning point in the development both of the division as a working community and of the philosophy of participative management.

12 The Review

It was clear from early on that an attempt should be made to evaluate the whole exercise, but that it would be a difficult and possibly inconclusive task. We decided that, as there were so many competing interests to be considered in any evaluation, a group covering most of these interests should be established.

We therefore set about establishing a group to consider what should be done. At the first meeting the agenda was:

    i.   the constitution of the group;

    ii.   the objectives of the review;

    iii.   how we go about it - the options and constraints.

Representatives from the management team, the unions, Staff Development Branch and the various Reference Groups were invited to attend, and a brief paper from us on the possible aims objectives and structure of the evaluation was circulated beforehand. The main point we wanted to make was that evaluation might be quite inappropriate as a title since it raised ideas about measurement and quantification which might be impracticable when dealing with issues like behaviour, the spread of ideas and individual perceptions of change. We therefore needed to be clear right from the start that much of the information we could gather would be subjective and descriptive and would probably not lend itself to any attempts at quantification.

We also underlined the conflicting interests involved in staging a review. An exercise of this kind might well generate a whole range of questions from a wide spectrum of interested parties present - all of whom could, and probably would, show legitimate interest in particular themes. But there had to be an overriding concern to keep the exercise relatively short and simple. This was appropriate to the stage which participative management had reached and to the resources available to carry out the evaluation or assessment. As far as we were concerned, our interest in a formal assessment centred around;

      a need to judge whether the diagnosis contained in our original report was correct,

      a need to find out whether the processes initiated through the participative management exercise had been effective.

      a need to enquire about our own style of operating as consultants, and a need to come to some conclusions about the extent and degree of any changes that had come about in job satisfaction, participation, managerial behaviour and organisational climate.

Other people or groups would have other needs and it would be part of the function of the Review Group to identify these needs and blend them into an integrated whole.

We also pointed at a range of as yet unanswered technical problems. A wide range of methods might be employed but the limited time and resources available cut down the field considerably. Eventually it was decided that the most appropriate method would be some kind of self-completion questionnaire comprising both multiple choice and open-ended questions to be given to all staff in Computer Division. Other suggestions had included a conference, a film and a simple three or four question survey. The question of collation and interpretation of the responses was going to be a tricky one. We did not wish to do it for our objectivity might well be suspect. Eventually it was agreed that a senior manager and a union officer would prepare the initial report which would be subjected to revision by the group as a whole.

The first problem that we encountered was a strong opposition from the unions to the membership of the committee. The grounds were that the unions, as elected and accredited representatives of the staff, should not share a forum of that kind with individual members of the staff who, however vaguely, were also expected to represent the interests of "the staff". This theme ran strongly through the whole business of designing and administering the review. It represented a new and stronger attitude on the part of the unions to the question of possible overlap and conflict between union representation through the normal Whitley machinery and participative management as an "alternative" process of joint consultation. The main problem was the view that participative management might undermine the unions' traditional bargaining and representative roles. The Review Group agreed to a limitation of the staff representative membership of the group to the elected trade union members, but reserved the right to employ other members of the staff who wished to help with the review in any capacity that seemed appropriate.

The process from then on was fairly straightforward. Each interested group contributed lists of ideas for issues to be investigated and questions to be asked and, with some professional help from a member of Social Survey Division an agreed questionnaire gradually emerged. It contained twenty questions and broadly attempted to find out what people felt were the aims of the exercise and to what extent they had been achieved, what changes had occurred as a result of the participative management initiative, how the exercise had affected them personally, how they saw its effect on the division as a whole and how (and if) they would like to see it develop in the future.

The next major difficulty concerned the administration of the survey. The unions' continuing and strongly held view was that the questionnaire should be distributed by them only to their members since the unions were the only appropriate and legitimate vehicle for seeking the views of the staff as a whole. This view had been reinforced by discussions during visits to the office by full-time national union officers. The principle was hotly debated in the Review Group but the unions were unyielding in their view and emphasised that their membership fully supported this stance. In the end, in the interests of carrying out the review at all, the other constituents of the group agreed to the proposal.

The reaction from the staff as a whole to this decision to limit the questionnaire to union members only was quite marked and was encapsulated in an open letter to the Review Group from members of the staff in Programming, Planning and Service Branches. It indicated that the local union leaders certainly did not enjoy the support of the majority of their members on the particular issue of 'members only'. The letter stated:

"the questionnaire issued by the Review Group should have been circulated to all members of Computer Division as all members were invited to be involved in participative management. We feel the questionnaire will not give a true picture because some people will not complete the form - due to annoyance rather than apathy, and also because a 100% poll of Computer Division is not being taken.

On this issue, we feel that unions are not representing our views and we are anxious that the Review Group should be aware of this fact. Nevertheless, while we think participative management should provide a general forum for relevant issues, members are aware that certain matters require union consultation and these must be channelled accordingly."

The point made about staff annoyance causing non-completion of the form seemed to have some merit when the final response to the questionnaire was evaluated eg:

Staff in post - 318.

Forms issued (to union members only) - 258

Forms returned - 150

ie forms were issued to 81.4% of the total staff; were received back from 47.2% of total staff, or 58.1% of forms issued were returned.

In fact, the overall rather low level of response was due in large measure to the very poor response from the clerical and data processing areas; the response from the executive grades was reasonably satisfactory. Figure 6 gives the distribution of the responses by grade and branch.

It was clear that some people did not reply because of their reaction to the way the questionnaire was administered, but the low overall response was due as much, if not more, to other factors such as the lack of experience of participative management in some areas, and the apathy which still existed in parts of the office.

FIGURE 6: RESPONSE TO REVIEW QUESTIONNAIRE

Grade	No in post (17 12 76)	No in union	No replied	replies % No in post	replies % No in union
Executive					
Senior +	31	30	22	70.9	77.3
Middle	49	45	34	69.4	75.5
Junior	93	70	53	56.9	75.7
Clerical	47	27	16	34.0	59.3
Data Processor	98	86	25	25.5	29.1
TOTALS	318	258	150	47.2	58.1

Branch	No in post (17 12)	No in union	No replied	replies % No in post	replies % No in union
DEV Gp (Programming Planning Service)	115	97	69	60.0	71.4
Production	144	115	45	31.25	39.1
S Survey (London	32	24	21	65.5	87.5
Rest (Resource T&SD Methods)	27	22	15	55.5	68.2
TOTALS	318	258	150	47.2	58.1

A concilliatory reply was made by the Review Group to the open letter:

"We have been made aware of the feelings of many of the staff of Computer Division on this issue, both by comments made in the returned questionnaires and by approaches made by individuals to members of the Review Group. Your letter confirms the general mood.

It is obviously impractical to start again, but the views of respondents on this particular issue are being noted and will be summarised in an appropriate part of the final report. We hope that the dissatisfaction you refer to in your final paragraph will not prevent people from completing the questionnaire and making any comments on the administration of the review that they may think fit. In this way, the success of the review will be assured whilst the strength of the general concern about the arrangements for the distribution of the questionnaire will be properly reported and recorded."

It was clear that the strength of reaction from the staff at large had been underestimated by the unions, but all agreed, including to their great credit the union officers, that this, in itself, was useful learning about the attitudes and feelings of union members about the role and purpose of their union.

The Report of the Review Group

This proved a fascinating document. We had had no particular influence on its contents and findings which were agreed by both management and union representatives on the group to be objective and impartial. The document itself was quite long and detailed (as was inevitable, it being a close analysis of about 150 questionnaires each with 20 questions) and it would be inappropriate to give a full account of the findings here. However, some of the salient points to emerge are recorded in the following paragraphs.

First, the response to the questionnaire was somewhat disappointing. 258 forms were distributed but only 150 usable replies were returned. Figure 6 shows the percentage of respondents from branches and grades. It was clear that data processors and clerical staff were under-represented in the coverage of the division, as was Production Branch. However, the Review Group felt that there were sufficient respondents from all areas to cover a wide range of views and it seemed probable that the results were representative of the views of the staff in the various grades and areas involved.

Secondly, an early question attempted to establish what the aims of the exercise had been. Most people thought that the two main aims of the exercise were "to involve the staff in decision making, to involve them more in their work etc" and "to improve or increase job satisfaction". In addition to being asked to state the aims of the exercise, staff were asked to grade the aims by degree of importance and extent of achievement. 73% of the aims were thought to be very important and 66% of those were thought to have been achieved (to some extent (58%) or to a great extent (8%). The two main aims, "involvement" and "job satisfaction", were thought to have been achieved to some or a great extent in 71% and 62% of the answers respectively.

Referring to the extent to which people felt that the exercise had led to changes, the results showed that while overall 52% of the respondents thought that there had been lasting changes, only 20% of the data preparation girls and 27% of the clerical staff thought this. Over half the junior and middle executive grades thought that there had been changes and even more of the senior staff thought so. The report asked "Can it be that change is more obvious the further away you are from the main working levels, or were the changes not made uniformly throughout the grades?" There were 56 people who were in Computer Division before participative management was introduced who stated that there had been no noticeable change or that changes had now vanished. Of these 48 gave a total of 65 reasons why this was so. Nearly one-third of the answers indicated that "management's reluctance to change" was the main reason for lack of change. It is noticeable that Production Branch and the smaller branches were the areas where participative management was thought to have existed before it was officially introduced.

Job satisfaction was a key issue in the Review and the results were mildly disappointing to us. Although 71% of the most senior managers thought that their job satisfaction had changed for the better as a direct result of participative management, this contrasted strongly with the senior grades where only 25% thought that participative management had increased their job satisfaction. Less than half the junior (44%) and the middle grades (39%) thought likewise. The report concluded that with the exception of 32 people, there had been little change in job satisfaction in Computer Division as a whole as a result of participative mangement.

Questions concerning the degree of involvement in the activity showed that there had been a marked increase in participation the higher the position in the hierarchy, with middle grade involvement at 59% and senior grade involvement at 68%. The report concluded that it was not clear whether this was due to greater opportunity or greater willingness, but it did show that participative management was not involving people evenly across the board in its formal groups. It was interesting to note that when the questions concerning the degree of involvement and the level of improvement of job satisfaction were cross-referenced it became clear that the most satisfaction was achieved by those who participated most. We considered this a reassuring finding; which to some extend countered our disappointment with the overall job satisfaction assessment.

Comments on our role in the exercise were ambiguous, with comments being divided almost equally between the view that we were guilty of "trying to impose their own ideas" and "they should have provided more guidance". We were not quite sure how to interpret the comment "they always agree with everything you say - usually before you say it"!

On the overall assessment of the exercise, 39% of respondents felt that the exercise had been "good for me", and 45% felt that it had been "valuable to

Computer Division" (in both categories the "bad for me" and "harmful for Computer Division" response was 9%). In the breakdowns by branch only 27% of Production Branch found it valuable to themselves or Computer Division and a breakdown into areas showed that this could not be totally attributed to the data preparation area where participative management was introduced fairly late. In the other branches there was quite a difference between the number who thought it valuable to Computer Division (60%) and who thought it a good thing for themselves (40%). The report suggested that this might be attributable to the fact that these branches tended to be the small ones where an informal atmosphere was more likely to have already existed. In the breakdowns by grade there could be seen a big spread in the percentage who found it a good thing personally (24% of Data Preparation to 75% of the top managers) and an even larger spread in those who thought it valuable to Computer Division (20% data preparation to 87% top management). The report suggested that the higher percentages at the top level might be attributable to the fact that they had been involved in participative management from the start and might feel more commitment to it than the lower grades.

The authors of the report felt that certain themes emerged strongly from their analysis of the questionnaires. One of these was to do with union involvement in participative management. It was clear from the comments that many union members felt strongly that participative management had little to do with traditional union areas of activity and equally that other union members saw participative management as infringing on their territory and being less than democratic in its operation. The combined union view was that during the course of the exercise it became apparent that participative management could involve a great deal more work for union representatives, over and above their normal commitments. In retrospect it was obvious that the unions needed to spell out the reasons for their policy of "wait and see" and to communicate more effectively with their members. The union representatives found that the increase in their workload brought about by participative management was the proverbial last straw, and it soon became obvious to them that they could not spend the same amount of time on participation as management, partly as a result of some union representatives working outside Computer Division and on other jobs, and partly because some senior management were spending a good deal of their time on the exercise. This, it was felt, led to misunderstandings between union officers and their constituents in Computer Division.

A second theme to emerge was that concerning the role of management in the exercise. Over 50% of the people giving reasons for lack of changes gave "management's reluctance to change" as their answer. It would appear that the top managers were not always successful in communicating with their more junior staff or in ensuring that changes in style or attitude occurred. In defence of the managers the authors of the report suggested that it was not easy even for the most committed people to change habits acquired over a period of years, and lapses were only to be expected. In some cases, of course, the staff's resistance to change was also apparent. Another important problem which seemed to have for themselves (40%). The report suggested that this might be attributable to the fact that these branches tended to be the small ones where an informal atmosphere was more likely to have already existed. In the breakdowns by grade there could be seen a big spread in the percentage who found it a good thing personally (24% of Data Preparation to 75% of the top managers) and an even larger spread in those who thought it valuable to Computer Division (20% data preparation to 87% top management). The report suggested that the higher percentages at the top level might be attributable to the fact that they had been involved in participative management from the start and might feel more commitment to it than the lower grades.

The authors of the report felt that certain themes emerged strongly from their analysis of the questionnaires. One of these was to do with union involvement in participative management. It was clear from the comments that many union members felt strongly that participative management had little to do with traditional union areas of activity and equally that other union members saw participative management as infringing on their territory and being less than democratic in its operation. The combined union view was that during the course of the exercise it became apparent that participative management could involve a great deal more work for union representatives, over and above their normal commitments. In retrospect it was obvious that the unions needed to spell out the reasons for their policy of "wait and see" and to communicate more effectively with their members. The union representatives found that the increase in their workload brought about by participative management was the proverbial last straw, and it soon became obvious to them that they could not spend the same amount of time on participation as management, partly as a result of some union representatives working outside Computer Division and on other jobs, and partly because some senior management were spending a good deal of their time on the exercise. This, it was felt, led to misunderstandings between union officers and their constituents in Computer Division.

A second theme to emerge was that concerning the role of management in the exercise. Over 50% of the people giving reasons for lack of changes gave "management's reluctance to change" as their answer. It would appear that the top managers were not always successful in communicating with their more junior staff or in ensuring that changes in style or attitude occurred. In defence of the managers the authors of the report suggested that it was not easy even for the most committed people to change habits acquired over a period of years, and lapses were only to be expected. In some cases, of course, the staff's resistance to change was also apparent. Another important problem which seemed to have affected several of the management grades was that of adjusting to the changed role that participative management seemed to demand. With the lower grades becoming more involved in decision making the need for a distinction between different executive and management grades sometimes was thought to have become somewhat blurred. In some cases they had seen themselves as by-passed or ignored in the decision making processes. However, experience of this varied between the various areas and could have been due as much to the personalities affected several of the management grades was that of adjusting to the changed role that participative management seemed to demand. With the lower grades becoming more involved in decision making the need for a distinction between different executive and management grades sometimes was thought to have become somewhat blurred. In some cases they had seen themselves as by-passed or ignored in the decision making processes. However, experience of this varied between the various areas and could have been due as much to the personalities involved as to participative management itself. The question of commitment too was important. Half-hearted or cynical partial acceptance of participation was seen by several people to be an issue of real importance. It was felt that participative management would only work if accepted wholeheartedly by all involved. Similarly there was felt to be a need for re-affirmation of commitment to participation and a fresh impetus to be given at regular intervals. The underlying problem would seem to be that there was a risk of participation tending to disappear if those chiefly concerned in promulgating it were allowed to revert to their former ways. Old habits died hard.

The report used quotations quite freely to give a flavour of the kind of responses given in the questionnaires. Despite the problems, difficulties and disappointments that had been reported there was still a considerable undercurrent of favourable comment about participative management and some of the quotations were particularly gratifying:

> "I fully support the concept of participation and wish it to continue. I believe that the participative management era is here to stay for a considerable period and has certainly been successful in Programming Branch."

> "There is a greater feeling of unity amongst the staff, rather than the "us" "them" situation which prevailed before. Senior management is far more approachable. . . . . there is a greater feeling of involvement among staff. . . "

> "It has given me the opportunity to "grow" considerably as a manager and to gain new insights into the management of people, work and organisations."

> ". . . I hope in any other post I will have the chance to air my opinions as I am encouraged to do at present. For this reason I hope that participative management will continue."

The conclusions reached in the report are probably worth quoting in full:

> "Considering firstly the overall effects of participative management on Computer Division it seems right to conclude that the exercise so far has been worthwhile. However, while a substantial number of people have felt it to be a good thing for them, an equal number, and this is perhaps surprising, have been unaffected by participation. While improving the lot of some of the staff, participative management is

also seen by a majority of the staff who expressed an opinion to have been valuable to Computer Division itself.

A second conclusion is that the introduction of participative management and its initial implementation was less than perfect. The criticisms of the managers and of the external consultants team point to this and it seems that many people, excluding of course the top management, felt that they were left too long in a state of uncertainty as to what the precise aims of the exercise and the intentions of the managers were. Some people would have preferred a scheme to have been put before them at the outset in which the roles of the various grades and parts of the organisation were carefully described. Civil servants expect rules and regulations.

Participative management will change continuously and no one formal, or informal, system will be right for all areas of Computer Division at any one time. While the aims and objectives should remain constant great flexibility must be allowed in the manner in which they are achieved. However, the lack of a 'system' could lead to the disappearance of participation in some areas. This suggests that a responsibility should be placed somewhere in the organisation to monitor the existence of participative management and to help staff to reactivate it if they wish to do so.

It may not be right to attribute all the improvements which have occurred in Computer Division since the introduction of participation to participative management itself. After the fragmentation of the pre Computer Division organisations and their subsequent amalgamation into new units there was bound to be a period of unrest followed by a settling in period during which new bonds were formed. With or without participation time should have eased some of the problems.

Experience of participative management has varied between the various areas and grades. In general the lower grades and the areas where most of them work have been least affected."

Similarly, the recommendations of the report are also worth quoting in their entirety;

"Participative management should continue in areas where the staff involved think it appropriate.

The time is ripe for some definitions of participative management to be published. The aims of participative mangement as disclosed by this review backed up by a statement of the management's objectives would be the minimum desirable.

A method must be found as soon as possible whereby participative management can work happily without alienating the unions, their members,or Personnel Branch and without prejudicing national or local union ('Whitley'), agreements. It ought to be possible to produce a set of guidelines entitled 'Participative management and the unions' which would be acceptable to all sides locally.

The Staff Development Branch should remain involved in the organisation of participative management. The section should be responsible for monitoring, at a low level, participative management activity and all staff should have the right, and know that they have the right, to consult with Staff Development Branch if they have problems with the organisation (or existence) of participation in their areas. The Staff Development Branch management must ensure that staff allocated to this work do not become either apathetic or too involved in the problems under discussion.

Managers at all levels should ensure that *all* their staff are still aware of participative management and that they can participate if they wish. If participation is to be introduced elsewhere then more thought should be given to the method of introduction. In particular the promulgators need to be fairly explicit as to what participative management is, or could be, and they should ensure that all levels of management are involved before a scheme is introduced."

The reader must draw his own conclusions from all this. In our view these results were remarkably encouraging, coming less than a year after the participative process had been commenced. They showed that the advantages and benefits were clearly recognised, even though the inevitable problems and shortcomings were also much in evidence. There seemed to exist a genuine goodwill towards the processes we had initiated and only a handful of people (perhaps no more than nine or ten) wanted to revert to former practices. There were clearly some major flaws but it seemed to us that the recommendations of the group had touched on two of the most acute, the need for a clearer definition of what participative management meant, and the establishing of a 'modus vivendi' with the unions. We decided that we would be more than content if the next step in the development of participative management in the organisation was to tackle these two key issues. We felt that the Review Group report itself was a remarkable piece of organisational learning about its own behaviour and was a healthy sign for the future development of the Division.

13 A Definition of Participation

One of the main recommendations arising from the review was that a clear definition of participation should be produced. In this Chapter we set out as precisely as possible how we perceived the basic characteristics of our intervention strategy. In that we believed this strategy had to be consistent with our philosophy of participation, this will provide an introduction to our definition of the participative process.

This attempt to capture the essence of the participative process and to concisely express it has been a difficult task. We began without a pre-conceived plan but later developed some half formed ideas based largely on the diagnostic exercise. In the event these ideas, together with those of the people with whom we worked, and the events of the project merged to form an experience which has largely determined the nature of the analysis that follows.

Two main arguments appear to be advanced to support a participative approach to management. These may be called:-

    (1)   the outcomes argument

    (2)   the humanistic argument

The outcomes argument views participation more as a mechanism or a technique which can facilitate more productive organisational behaviour. For instance all large industrial organisations experience some degree of inter-group conflict. Participation may be presented as a method of breaking down the barriers between antagonistic groups by establishing or improving communication. This can facilitate an understanding of each other's problems and lead to the development of more harmonious relationships.

Participation may also be depicted as a technique for tapping the abilities of many more people in the organisation who might otherwise, because of prescribed patterns of interaction, be denied an opportunity to contribute. The organisation can benefit from both this contribution and the improved feedback which results.

These sorts of potential organisational benefits have been advanced as the main rationale for forms of indirect participation such as coopting workers onto the managing board. The idea seems to be that conflict between the management group and the workers, the "them and us" syndrome, will be reduced by altering the constitution of the controlling group and allowing representatives of those at lower organisational levels a voice in the policy making decisions. The crucial question for the success of this strategy we believe will be whether or not there will be sufficient behavioural change in the newly constituted managing groups to satisfy the forces which have produced the pressure for change.

Even at this basic level of analysis it is possible to see that in order to attain the projected beneficial outcomes it is necessary to create more flexibility in the organisation and to develop a more democratic climate. This can prove quite threatening to those exercising more conventional forms of control. Certainly in the earlier days of the project we tended to portray participation in these outcome terms and were surprised at the strength of reaction from some people. Our message was something to the effect that by facilitating communication and allowing staff at all levels to be able to influence their working life it was likely that people would be more satisfied and organisational performance would improve.

On reflection it is apparent that we tended to stress the possible beneficial outcomes of participation rather than the deeper reasons for such a programme that we have called the humanistic argument. One reason for this emphasis was simply that it is much harder to express a philosophy of participation which embraces the deeper human issues, in words. When one tries it often sounds either trite or excessively idealistic and out of touch with reality. Though at an intellectual level we found senior management accepting a philosophical argument for more participation, at a behavioural level the necessary support was not always forthcoming. Enid Mumford [1] has noted the same phenomenon. It is possible that our tendency to present participation as a technique encouraged the cynical view among the staff that we were the agents of a management who were primarily interested in improving productivity.

We believe that there is no easy way out of this dilemma facing the interventionist. If he stresses beneficial outcomes he tends to be viewed as being involved in a management con. If he adopts a more philosophical approach, for instance stressing the sort of features we give an impressionistic description of in Chapter 1, he may be accused of being out of touch with the reality of getting the job done.

The way out of this dilemma is quite simply by letting people experience for themselves that the participative process can be something other than a management con. This can only be convincing if the staff at all levels feel that they have ownership of the process. In short they must do it for themselves. It was necessary for the intervention strategy we adopted to be consistent with this ideal and it is to this that we now turn.

We have examined some of the theoretical and empirical literature on intervention strategy and some of this links fairly closely with our perception of the role. An American psychologist Weick [2] has suggested that rather than regarding the process of organising as a transformation of raw materials into finished products, information and meaning are the central commodities upon which organisations operate. An item of information contains several possibilities and implications. If action is to be taken then the equivocal properties of the message must be made more unequivocal. (For instance in the topic structure discussions people and groups of people were subjected to a flow of information which was capable of various interpretations.) Weick suggests

96

that organising is a process where equivocal inputs come into the system, (or can be internally generated), and are first registered and then dealt with by processes which vary in the amount of equivocality they remove. He argues that for equivocal information to be registered and handled it must be dealt with in an equivocal manner. Most management consultants do not deal with equivocal information in an equivocal way; they often employ a set of particular techniques to sort out problems. Such an approach seems likely to touch on only a small part of the problem and would be likely to leave much of the equivocality untouched. Analysing organisations in terms of information and meaning does not of course lead inevitably to the conclusion that a participative approach to managing is the most appropriate. In fact Weick goes on to question the whole principle of participation. He develops a model of organisations which relies on adaptive responses for survival in a changing environment. He argues that conflict and polarised view-points aid the adaptive process. In that participation is likely to reduce the range of responses and lead to convergency and compromise, long-term adaptability will be destroyed. It can also be argued that, because of the nature of the authority structure in hierarchical organisations, the range of responses - though possibly polarised - is narrow in that important decisions are taken only by the top management team. We would argue that a fully participative learning process can actually broaden the range of responses. Participation does not necessarily reduce the range of adaptive responses; participation is about sharing decisions and this does not necessarily imply narrow compromise. In fact the experience of this project suggested that the relationships and decision making structures that were established led to a greater likelihood that issues were dealt with in an equivocal way.

What we see of particular relevance in Weick's concept of equivocality is the apparently obvious feature that where you have a flow of equivocal informational inputs, different people will interpret the meaning of those inputs according to their particular situation and experience. This creates a political situation among the various interests involved. This political dimension has not been given the attention it warrants in most of the management literature.

These different interests present in organisational life, rooted in the individual or groups of individuals, exist with various degrees of tension. The state of tension can change over time and is indicated by such phenomena as open hostility between individuals or groups or the creation of temporary coalitions of interests. An external interventionist can usefully picture his work in an organisation as attempting to bring together several client groups comprising many individual clients, all in different states of political tension, into a harmonious working relationship. This harmony depends on the clients being able to recognise the political reality around them and being prepared to learn to handle it. The political character of organisational life implies that each interest has a power base and this is a crucially important element. Thus, achieving a more effective working harmony implies an ability to recognise the power base of each interest and a willingness to try to put aside any manipulation of the other, (or at least to recognise when it is happening), and to work as individuals in groups who have particular skills and abilities to contribute to achieving mutually worthwhile goals which are recognised as such.

A European organisational psychologist Vansina [3] suggests that the interventionist should attempt to develop a relationship with all the clients. "The relationship is one of joint effort where there is a mutual determination of goals and in which each party has equal opportunity to influence the other." The important characteristics of this approach are that the development process is organic and not mechanistic, and that the parties define areas where their divergent objectives and interests are compatible and where there is a room for joint optimisation. Note that it is the parties who define the areas of interest for themselves, no one does it for them. Secondly all the parties with a legitimate interest are involved. It is this characteristic of the people involved doing things for themselves which we believe is the key to a successful participation programme. This approach can be compared with two other models discussed by Vansina -

> *The client-centred model*. Here, the client, usually senior management, determines what they want to do and the consultant helps implement proposals eg a job enrichment exercise.

> *The consultant-centred model*. Here the consultant formulates specific proposals after an investigatory phase and presents a report for implementation - usually just before "taking the next 707 out of town!"

An Americal psychologist Argyris [4] analyses the structure of the "psychological contract" implicit in the above process. The term "psychological contract" refers to the set of expectations the employee has of the organisation and the set of expectations the organisation has of employees. Since an organisation consists of people interacting one with another the contract refers to relationships between people. He says these should be characterised by the generation of valid information, the free and informed choice by the client system, and the internal commitment by the parties concerned with implementation. In practice there are problems. Free and informed choice is easy to say but not easy to achieve when the starting point within the organisation is very distant from the ideal. Internal commitment is unlikely to be given unanimously or unequivocally. In short, though admirable as ultimate aims, these statements can lead to over-optimism and idealism and not to recognition of the political reality which in fact the interventionist faces.

The "doing it yourself" philosophy is something of a half-way house between two other extreme approaches; the purely academic/theoretical and the traditional commercial consultants approach. Whereas the academic approach may involve clinical experimentation without full participation of all the parties concerned, and the commercial consultants approach may depend on the imposition of a predetermined solution to a pre-identified problem, the do-it-yourself approach invests the thought and action within all levels of the organisation. In a very real sense the external agent does not know what is going to happen (learning is impossible if you start out knowing the answer!). The interventionist brings a philosophy of self-help which by its very nature will lead to a more gradualistic approach to change than does traditional consultancy. (This gradualism raises questions for evaluation. The time-scale for real attitudinal change and the development of a learning orientation is likely to be years rather than months. Evaluation of such consultant activity in terms of strict cost and tangible benefits is likely to produce at best only a partial answer.)

Our own learning since the beginning of participative management was significant. At the beginning, we were certainly somewhat idealistic and theoretical about the whole process. We lacked knowledge and understanding of the practical realities. Even the experience we did have was not particularly relevant to an ADP environment. After our practical experience we saw things somewhat differently. We would sum up our view towards the end of the project as follows. Any adaptive process requires that the organisation is able to learn from its mistakes. This means making effective use of the knowledge and experience that is constantly being accumulated at all levels of the organisation. The difficulty is how to make this learning process a natural feature of organisational life. An organisation can be interpreted as a network of intertwined vested interests which can vary over a range from the intensely selfish to the heroically altruistic. These interests create the political environment within which organisational activity takes place. It is necessary to try to overcome the differences inherent in such a situation. Our contributions towards defining participation is as follows:

"Participation is an outward manifestation of a philosophy about how people ought to behave towards each other in an ideal state. An expression of freedom, equality and adult relationships. In the western post-industrial world we live in, we believe the demand for these kind of human relationships is growing. *BUT* it is an imperfect world we live in. Fixed attitudes exist, human variations, economic, social psychological pressures exist and all combine to produce a very uneven and imperfect environment. Perfect representation, complete participation and fully unanimity about decisions are impossible to achieve so that concensus around a compromise and give and take are the nearest we can get to the perfect state; people being what they are will always be dissatisfied or want something different (and it is good that they should). So that in striving towards an ideal philosophy in an imperfect world the most we can hope for is a shift in attitudes, a movement in thinking and some change in behaviour.

Although the statement "let people do things for themselves" appears simple and rational, it is deceptively so; consultancy based on this philosophy is full of pitfalls and difficulties. How do you get people to take responsibility for their own learning? Is such an approach possible at all given the existing hierarchical relationships, rigid role definitions and restricted access to information that exists in tradititional bureaucracies where caution and delay create massive inertia and opposition to change? Is it possible to develop consultative relationships and trust in such an environment?

We soon discovered that what we were trying to achieve was a radical shift of values within an environment which exhibited some of the pathological features of the old traditional bureaucracies - features which were fundamentally opposed to the kind of behavioural change we wanted to see. We could not overthrow the old bureaucratic system but felt that we were working towards a new kind of organisation which linked the experience and wisdom of the old with the promise and energy of the future. We called it "the New Bureaucracy".

NOTES

[1]   Mumford, E. and Jacmkan, H; "Human Choice and Computers" North Holland, 1974

[2]   Weick K, "The Social Psychology of Organising" Addison Wesley 1969

[3]   Vansina, L.S., "Beyond Organisation Development". Paper presented to NATO conference on Goals, Values and Work, University of York, 1974

[4]   Argyris, C; "Intervention Theory and Method" Addison Wesley, 1970

14 Essential Features and Guidelines for the New Bureaucracy

In this chapter we discuss the degree of success achieved in this project in developing the distinguishing features of the new bureaucracy. These features were:

The style of management

The management of change

The working of the organisation

We then draw some more general conclusions about the process which can serve as guidelines to any organisation undertaking such a change programme.

The factor common to each of these features and unifying them all was the participative philosophy. In the final chapter we therefore broaden the perspective to consider the rationale for participation in some depth, and what we learned at we learned about it. Finally we focus on the key issue of the desire for participation amongst the work force.

Most of these conclusions are judgements based on our own feelings and are not strongly supported by hard evidence. The reader must therefore make his own assessment of their validity based on the evidence of the preceding chapters, on what he knows of society and his own experience of work.

The Style of Management and the Management of Change

It is sensible to take these two themes together as aspects of the same issue. In the diagnosis we tried to paint a picture of an organisation in which a particular kind of staff - young, well qualified and with high expectations about work - were being managed in an inappropriate way - remotely, hierarchically, formally and with little opportunity for direct involvement. This is in some ways a caricature of the situation but it is necessary to depict it so in order to illustrate the point that to improve job satisfaction and effectiveness the management climate needed to be modified. We proposed direct participation as the vehicle by which this might be achieved. The suggestion that management style needed to be modified to make it more appropriate to the staff employed, and to the turbulent environment in which they worked, was a fundamental part of the philosophy. It was a broad value judgement based on our interpretation of social trends linked with the evidence we collected. Was this judgement valid; did the style of management change, and, if it did, are things better because of it? It needs to be said straight away that we have no conclusive proof either that the style of management, however defined, has changed, or if it has changed, things are "better". As Foy and Gadon comment [1] "the fuzzy costs and benefits of participative programmes make the "soft sciences" much harder to evaluate" than the harder technologies of the past". We can however make some informed judgements from the results of the review and from our general observations.

For instance, nearly half of the respondents to the review felt that there had been permanent changes in the way in which their branch worked as a result of the participative management exercise; well over half the respondents identified some greater involvement of staff in decision making as a major aim of the exercise and most of these felt that this aim had been achieved to some or a great extent. Nearly a third of respondents, too, felt that there had been a change for the better in the way in which Computer Division handled change.

A phenomenon familiar to social researchers is the difficulty experienced by interviewees in recalling the nature and quality of change which has been lived through. Thus, questions seeking to identify changes, particularly changes in subtle things like relationships and attitudes, are notoriously difficult to answer. Our own subjective judgement, based mainly on observation of senior managers at work, on the experience of the second workshop, on the way that the subsequent changes have been handled, and on the way the major new branches are now working is that a significant change in behaviour has taken place at the top management level. The process is undoubtedly a long-term one and it should be remembered that we are talking here of reactions after less than a year.

It would be reasonable to claim therefore that quite significant changes in management style at top levels are beginning to work through the organisation, and are being recognised. In some areas there would be little chance of reverting to the old order but other areas of the Division have some way to go before a shift in style is established permanently. The final question, how valid was the judgement in the first place, is almost impossible to answer. Looking at it negatively, only a handful of people in the Division who responded to the questionnaire felt that the aims and processes of the participative management exercise and the changes brought about by it were positively harmful; the rest were more or less equally divided between those who were generally in favour of what had happened, and saw good in it, and those who were neutral or who had been little affected by it. One of the more positive indicators that the move has been in the right direction was provided by cross referencing certain questions in the questionnaire to show that 40% of those who have been involved in participative management group activities reported that their job satisfaction had been improved as a result. Only 6% felt the experience had worsened their job satisfaction. The general conclusion must be that the judgement itself is still not proven, though the indications are that the changes in management style have been positive and have been recognised as broadly beneficial. A more conclusive assessment is probably impossible to make at this stage.

The Working of the Organisation

Once again, it may be that a conclusion on this complex matter would be premature. There is no doubt that much of the effect of the various reference and special interest groups was focused on issues to do with the working and functioning of the organisation. The Topic Orientation Group was the prime example and the repercussions of this group's work and the decision to restructure the organisation are too immediate to be assessable yet. But other groups looked at and successfully dealt with the whole range of interbranch working issues. It is also important to notice that respondents to the questionnaire cited "improving the efficiency and working of the organisation" and "improving communications" as being the third and fourth most frequently stated reasons for the exercise. A quarter of the respondents thought that there had been a change for the better in working relationships between branches. Undoubtedly the organisation has changed substantially as a direct result of the participative management exercise - and in a way which is likely, by the very nature of the change, to promote employee involvement and participation. It remains to be seen in the long term whether the change is going to be as important in terms of efficiency and effectiveness, though an indication may be gleaned from the fact that the users have welcomed the change.

Some Conclusions about the Change Process

Our first conclusion is an obvious one and applies to any kind of change process in an organisation. It is none the less a valuable one. It is essential to have the active support of the top man, not just at an intellectual level, but practically as well. He must be seen to be providing support by his direct involvement, by his encouragement and support, particularly in the field of providing moral backing to his managers in the matter of risk taking and by taking risks himself. The form this takes will depend on the individual personality of the man at the top, but the more visible he is to the majority of his staff the more valuable his contribution.

The role of the senior and middle managers is important. The strains and problems of participation fall most heavily on this group. They will recognise that they have most to lose in terms of status, power and their own investment in the system, and least to gain in terms of satisfaction, performance and control. They need to be convinced of the real benefits to the organisation as a whole of an active, involved and satisfied staff. They need to be coached on the different style they have to play. This is perhaps the most difficult part of the whole process since their role is changed from a directing to a predominantly supporting one. In such a position they are valued for the knowledge, experience and contribution they can make rather than for their status and position in the hierarchy. They remain ultimately accountable, but forgo their former unilateral control. This can be painful and sometimes a disturbing experience.

The role of the unions too is crucial. The agreement of the unions is an essential ingredient for the success of participation. The extent of their involvement is dependent on their understanding of what this process involves, so there is an important educational task for the consultant here. Their position is in many ways analogous to that of the managers, since they, too, can be seen to be at risk. They too have problems of communication and remoteness from their constituents, and they also have a need to control their membership. Processes which encourage greater freedom of action and more self-expression for their members can be interpreted by the unions as a move to undermine their authority and to breach the integrity of their bargaining and negotiating position.

On the other hand, the democratic traditions of unionism would, in theory, lend support to any move which tended to bring closer ties between the elected union officer and his membership. There can, therefore, be a dilemma for the union in, on the one hand, encouraging a process which would weaken their power base, or, on the other hand discouraging a process which reinforces the basic democratic tenets of trade unionism. Our conclusion would be that, brought into co-ownership of the process (the term "joint stewardship" was coined as a useful description of the concept), all unions will find the benefits will outweigh the risks. It is perhaps significant that one of the recommendations of the Review Group was that a method of working, agreeable to both management and unions, should be an early aim in the development of participative management.

Finally under this heading we think it important to comment on the creation of a set of institutions (the reference groups) which was an important element in demonstrating that a new way of working was being developed. The benefits of group activities of this kind in the early stages of the participative process are probably vital in any bureaucracy. But groups and meetings in themselves do not create a participative climate. True participation depends on attitudes and behaviour not on machinery and organisation. Groups are necessary as a forum for discussion, leading to change between established or discrete parts of an organisation. Ultimately, we would expect formal groups to be replaced by more open and participative methods of working within the normal hierarchy (the "New Bureaucracy", in fact), but group structures probably need to be retained for some time as alternatives for use when the conventional methods show themselves less adaptable.

The experience in Computer Division has taught us that the participative process is essentially evolutionary and developmental and is not immediately self-sustaining. In the early stages credibility is the major problem; widespread cynicism coupled with the lack of immediately visible benefits demand considerable staying power and courage on the part of those staff and managers who have openly committed themselves. Since the process is initially so difficult to initiate and sustain, the help of an external agent who is wholeheartedly committed to the philosophy and process, yet who is in organisational terms politically neutral, is of crucial importance.

The role of the outside agent is critical, and we do not believe that radical processes of this kind can be successfully launched without his assistance. His task has a variety of functions;

i.   Explaining the philosophy.

ii.   Developing some degree of commitment amongst key people by discussion and example.

iii.   Creating set piece situations to help the development of the process eg the two workshops, and also making constructive use of actual everyday events to aid learning.

iv.   Providing encouragement, support and advice, particularly at times of difficulty eg "hand holding" with managers when decisions are being taken by groups and they feel most vulnerable.

v.   Being a source of ideas and relevant experience from outside the organisation.

vi.   Maintaining the political neutrality of the project so that it becomes neither a platform for staff agitation nor managerial authoritarianism.

vii.   As impartial observer, acting as "go between" or facilitator between groups although *not* as an arbitrator.

viii.   Providing more positive help with staff who are inexperienced with group working, or who need assistance with committee procedures, drafting feedback and liaison work.

There is a fine balance to be drawn between the amount of positive help and direction the outside agent can provide and the preservation of his independent, impartial "facilitating" status. In Computer Division a combination of factors:

i.   The relative sophistication of most of the staff.

ii.   The degree of support from the top.

iii.   The wide front on which the exercise developed.

iv.   The impossibility in the time available of getting to grips with the complexities of the work and the technology.

v.   Our own strongly held view that we should principally "help people to do things for themselves".

moulded the low key style of our consultancy; but in another environment we can envisage an appropriate style which would be much more directive and interventionist. The consultant must, therefore, be able to assess what is the best kind of strategy to adopt, and be able to adapt and modify his contribution to meet the circumstances.

In Computer Division, we were able to use "third parties" from within the organisation to provide much the same kind of support - particularly for help with group meetings. This facet of consultancy is dealt with in some detail earlier and needs no further recapitulation here. Suffice it to say that third parties or internal consultants can play an important part in the development of the process, but they cannot fulfil all the tasks of the impartial external agent and their selection, training and development needs careful thought and attention.

These conclusions can be summed up in a number of guidelines:

1. It is essential to have the support of the man at the top.

2. The strains of participation, initially at any rate, will fall most heavily on senior and middle management who will require support.

3. The agreement and involvement of the unions is essential.

4. Some 'alternative' decision making machinery is probably necessary at least in the early stages, to allow junior staff to perceive a 'break out' from normal bureaucratic behaviour patterns.

5. Junior staff will be conservative and tend to appeal for direction.

6. An external agent committed to the philosophy is required. He must be politically neutral in order to handle attempts to manipulate other or further personal interests, to subdue group exclusiveness and to deal with inter personal problems. An internal consultant capacity should be developed.

7. Credibility will be an early problem, cynicism will be rife; endurance and an optimistic frame of mind are valuable assets.

NOTES

[1] Foy, N, and Gadon H; "Worker participation: contrasts in three countries", Harvard Business Review, Vol 55, No 3, May-June 1976.

15 Some Conclusions about the future of ADP work

Whilst most of our conclusions are general and we feel that they can be applied in broad areas of work, we cannot escape from the fact that we were working in the ADP world. Inevitably therefore we have some thoughts of the particular problems of an ADP environment. We have been influenced by a quotation from a paper entitled "Building Advanced Systems with Ordinary People" presented by F C Heward, Department of Education and Science, to the Government Computer Conference held at Church House on 12 and 13 March 1975. He said:

> "Today we are faced with the dilemma that we are trying to cope with machines of considerably higher power, scope and facility by using the services of people who appear to have more casual standards of achievement, service and motivation than those of yester-year."

Heward goes on to argue that an indivual's philosophy of life may be as important in determining his attitude to his work as all manner of pay and conditions of service, and that managers in ADP systems must become aware of this and adapt their style to suit the circumstances. During the diagnostic phase of the project, we repeatedly heard the adjectives "lethargic, apathetic and irresponsible" being used to describe the prevailing attitudes of programmers towards their work and the organisation - all were reminiscent of Heward's "casual standards of achievement, service and motivation". Psychologists believe that people react to frustration in a variety of ways. For instance, Vansina [1] has suggested that apathy, loss of identify and recoil to rigid individualism are well known reactions to frequent changes. It is possible that these sorts of reactions are responses to imposed change where people feel that they have no ownership of the change or knowledge of what is going to happen next. Other known reactions to frustration include aggression, regression and resignation and it seems to us that there exists within ADP work a potential for frustration among junior levels of staff that must be of concern to all who manage installations of this kind. The quotation from Heward's paper does not so much reflect the "ordinariness" of people in ADP organisations, as illustrate the outcome of inappropriate management styles or organisational regimes on young staff.

We consider, therefore, that there exist some major problems in the management of ADP work which would repay further attention:

> The frequency with which change occurs, particularly in the technological area, producing an unstable, turbulent working environment.

> The complexities of the technology seem to produce both fragmented, highly specialised jobs and over-simple, deskilled work.

The economies of scale in computer work seem to be producing large organisations, based on functionlisation and severe division of labour.

There is a concentration within ADP of relatively large numbers of young staff who have been well educated and whose values and culture are sometimes in conflict with those of their managers and the organisations within which they work.

The managers of ADP installations have generally been promoted rapidly within their technical field and are therefore comparatively inexperienced as managers. It seems likely, too, that people in ADP work are promoted more for their technical skills than for their managerial ability, which they get little opportunity to practice at the important early stages of their career. They also tend to bring with them a strong continuing interest in the technology and techniques of ADP work which may tend to relegate managerial considerations to positions of secondary importance in their minds.

We are convinced that the management of ADP work, because of the concentration and combination of these features, is a challenging and difficult task. But equally, we are not convinced that this has yet been sufficiently recognised. Too often the emphasis in training and development work in the public service is on the need to build up broad professional and specialist expertise, to maintain professional competence and to keep up to date with technical progress. There is virtually no reference to the need for managerial, as opposed to professional, ADP skills, and we believe this represents an imbalance in the planning for the future.

The same criticism can be applied to other areas of ADP work. For instance, the technical aspects of data preparation work get a great deal of attention in the literature, but little advice is given on its human problems. Maintaining a balance of concern between the technical and social components of a work system is an important part of any manager's task, and we believe that the experience and knowledge that may flow from an experiment of the kind we carried out in the Data Preparation area would provide help of a kind not available before to Data Preparation managers.

As we have suggested earlier, lasting improvements in job satisfaction are not easy to obtain and depend on more fundamental changes than improvements in environmental conditions alone. In addition to the question of developing an appropriate style of management for ADP work, other issues also seem important in this general field:

Is it an inescapable feature of the development of ADP technology and the economies of scale that "bigger is better", or are there benefits to be gained from the use of smaller computers which can be linked up for tasks requiring high levels of computing power but which require smaller human organisations to support them?

Even if some very large computers are needed, do their supporting organisation also have to be large? This brings to mind models of systems which incorporate the idea that many of the tasks usually associated with the computer system are properly the responsibility of the host system even down to areas such as systems analysis and design and possibly even programming.

Even if computers have to be large and their supporting organisations have to be big as well do they have to be designed on functional grounds which mean that groups of staff are isolated into organisational units responsible for only a part of the production process? We believe that in many ways this perpetuates the worst aspects of the flow line design philosophy, ignores developments in the fields of job design and group technology, and contributes to the feelings of apathy and purposelessness we found and which Heward referred to in his article. There is considerable evidence that organisational units having project responsibility for the whole production process provide more meaningful groupings for those working within them. Certainly in Computer Division this approach was preferred by the staff as a whole.

Whilst we accept the inevitable need for some degree of work specialisation, and believe that in many cases it can provide a sense of mastery over a subject and a good deal of job satisfaction we question the more extreme cases of this trend, as exemplified, for instance, in the technique known as Modular Programming. Do the cost savings claimed for this development justify the risks of staff dissatisfaction involved? These have already been well described in a guide entitled "Implications of Using Modular Programming" issued by the Central Computer Agency of the Civil Service[2]. We need only give one quotation from this guide:

> "The failure of Modular Programming in an installation was more often found to be the result of unpopularity with programmers than for any technical reasons."

We have chosen Modular Programming as an example because it is well documented. There are other examples of this kind of extreme specialistion which managers need to be concerned about.

The rapidity of change, which is inevitable in the ADP environment, brings problems for staff at all levels in assimilating new ideas, learning new techniques, adjusting to new ways of working and coping with different situations and stresses. Is enough attention being paid to ways of minimising these problems by training and helping managers to manage change itself?

One of the more disturbing trends we noticed during our study was the extent to which some managers, although becoming increasingly aware of job satisfaction issues, seemed to accept deterioration in levels of job satisfaction as an inevitable cost of improved economies or greater sophistication within ADP work. This unrelenting pursuit of economic goals was short-sighted and likely to be counter productive. A balanced attitude, such as we have outlined above seemed more likely to achieve lasting improvements.

NOTES

[1] Vansina, L.S., "Beyond Organisation Development. Paper presented to NATO Conference on Goals, Values and Work, University of York, 1974.

[2] Central Computer Agency Guide No 1, "Implications of using Modular Programming", HMSO, 1973.

16 The New Bureaucracy

It is a basic feature of our argument that the kind of organisation, working system and management style prevalent in the Civil Service, and we suspect other large bureaucracies, are out of step with the experience, expectations and life style of a growing proportion of the people who work in them. This mis-match is serious now and will grow more critical in the Civil Service as the great exodus of staff (as many as half in some departments), leaves on retirement in the next five to ten years. We believe that the Civil Service, and other large organisations, must adapt and change to meet the new challenge and that direct participation will have a great part to play in the process of adaptation towards "the new bureaucracy". Schein [1] stresses the importance for organisations of developing "assumptions about people that fit reality". The evidence on which these assumptions may be based is clear - we quote below, almost at random, from the wide range of reports, articles, books and documents that flood the market.

First, the Bullock report [2] commenting on social change:

> "New concepts of the role of employees in decision making at company level are not just reactions to economic trends. They also derive from social changes which have taken place since the war, especially rising standards of education and higher standards of living. The significance of the educational development is not just that more people have received a basic education; it is the nature of that education which has changed. There is now less concentration on formal authoritarian teaching methods and more encouragement for children to adopt independent and questioning approaches in order to develop individual initiative and adaptability. It is only since World War II that we have seen the end of the deferential society ..."

Another example of the theme of the changes in education can be drawn from "The Creighton Report", a description of a year in the life of a London comprehensive school by Hunter Davis [3], which gives a good impression of the values held by the young generation today:

> "The first thing I noticed about Creighton's senior pupils was their freedom. Compared with my day, the student is now free, more or less, to express himself, to make the school fit him rather than be fitted to the school. Equality and the rights of the individual are what matters ..." Also "They (the older pupils) are obsessed by not competing. It is considered anti-social to want to beat other people, a feeling which now appears to be universal in comprehensive sixth forms."

Generalising from both the previous book and from the paper dealing with attitudes towards authority prepared for the "Wider Issues Review", a study of broad issues affecting morale in the Civil Service and published in 1975, one could produce a list of some important attributes of the young people now coming into employment:

Informality - casualness, with less formal behaviour, speech and dress.

Egalitarian/democratic values - shown in a questioning and resentful attitude towards imposed authority and rules.

A studied non-competitiveness.

A caring and concerned approach to the problems of the under-privileged.

A creative frame of mind.

Independent and adventurous and anxious to exploit the world, yet, paradoxically, lacking in self confidence.

Both authors were mature students at new universities at the beginning of the 1970s. We felt that our fellow students were significantly more introverted, less competitive and more concerned with issues of a political and moral kind than our contemporaries in the late '50s had been.

Though these are broad generalisations and probably open to challenge, they are worth comparing with the characteristics thought to be necessary for the smooth functioning of bureaucracies, characteristics identified by Sofer [4].

A hierarchical structure with authority legitimised by established rules.

Functional structures with relationships between functions and hierarchical levels tending to be formal and rigid.

Within each functional area, strictly defined and relatively limited task structures.

Precise communication by means of the written word between functional areas.

A competitive environment, based on financial status and good quality job rewards.

A cold impersonal rather than a caring and concerned environment.

Though we are not suggesting public sector organisations, or large organisations in general, are necessarily characterised by all such conditions, most bureaucracies exhibit these features to some degree. There is clearly a significant disparity between the values generated in our educational system and those required by our organisations as presently constituted. Bureaucractic organisations tend to produce dependency on the system which increases with the time an individual spends in it. Doctor H. C. Coombs, Chairman of the Royal Commission on Australian Government Administration has been reported (the West Australian, 12 August 1976) as saying that public servants of long standing lack the enthusiasm and vitality of their younger colleagues. "Years of involvement in routine and ritualistic processes and a sense of isolation had destroyed their vitality and concern. The Australian Government Administration's defects lie principally in the way in which it is organised, in the impersonal style imposed on it and from the lack of scope for the men and women who compose it."

We believe from our study that the young ADP professional, independently minded, yet sometimes lacking in self confidence, may react similarly to his antipodean counterpart by "switching off" in the working environment which the Civil Service provides for him. In this project, therefore, our aim was to use the process of participation as a means of correcting the mismatch of organisation to expectations of staff. We felt that an organisation and style of management based on a free and questioning participative style would be more adaptable and would reflect more accurately a set of realistic assumptions about the staff employed in the office. Participation therefore was seen as an appropriate means to a particular end; a process by which the organisation and its style could be modified over time to more closely meet the needs of the staff. Miner [5] asks some pointed questions about participation as a management style. Advocates of the participative approach, he writes, have called for "... decentralisation ... expanded jobs ... the creation of temporary project teams ... more group decision making, the abolition of controlled procedures, increasing horizontal and two-way communication, acceptance structures rather than a formal authority structure and, above all else, greater equalisation of power throughout the organisation". He observes that this is a great deal for most existing managements to swallow (and we would wholeheartedly agree with him!) and he asks several key questions:

Will it work?

Can a company get its jobs done through participative management?

By creating participative structures to accommodate the motives and expectations of the young, do you waste the existing pool of managerial talent who are no longer "young"?

Are we substituting the "tyranny" of the majority for the "tyranny" of higher management?

Will participative management prove ponderous and slow, will it serve organisational goals, will it undermine co-ordination of efforts?

These all relate to the question *how* does participation work. Virtually all the features mentioned by Miner were present in this project. In the opening chapter we posed the question whether the "New Bureaucracy" can combine the freedom demanded by the emancipated worker with the discipline necessary for any co-operative undertaking. We believe our experience with the embryonic "new bureaucracy" at Computer Division, brief and imperfect as it may have been, has been a significant contribution to answering this fundamental question in the affirmative. Yes, participation works. Decisions take a bit longer, but it doesn't involve tyranny, it utilises managerial talent to a greater degree than previously and the organisational effectiveness does not suffer. The second fundamental question relates to whether employees will be prepared to participate given the existing climate of industrial relations. In the guidelines in Chapter 12 we indicated that cynicism about a participation programme would likely be rife. This kind of attitude is going to be difficult to overcome in a British industrial relations system described by Foy and Gadon [6] as "based on the adversary role of collective bargaining not the co-operative roles of participation". Generating the desire is vital to long term success. How then did the staff of Computer Division react to the opportunities offered for greater participation? It was our impression from the very early stage of the project that perhaps a third of the staff were switched on by the idea of participation and were committed in some measure to its success. This proved to be a fairly consistent proportion throughout the whole passage of the exercise, and our intuitive judgement was borne out, very closely, by the response to the Review. The Review also showed that staff in the higher grades felt that participative management had been far more valuable than staff in lower grades.

Two questions then follow naturally; why weren't more people turned on by the idea of participation; why was there such an apparent difference of attitude between machine operator grades and more highly qualified staff such as programmers and analysts? In the broad category of two thirds of the staff who we felt were not positively enthusiastic, a wide spectrum of attitudes seemed to emerge. The most frequently recurring were:

"We have participation already and don't want any new initiatives". This was common in all the smaller, more creative areas where the styles of the managers were already informal and participative.

"We want managers to manage, we want to be told what to do, managers should earn their money by taking decisions"; a fairly widespread philosophy though rather more strongly felt in some areas where a more formal and directive style was already practiced.

"Its all a management con, we don't want anything to do with it!";
cynicism and suspicion were very common right throughout the
exercise, though it was generally never extended to actual wrecking.

"What's it all about anyway; I don't understand it?"; for obvious reasons,
participative management was never standardised or categorised and
it was left very much to individuals to interpret the philosophy as
they wished. The variety of methods and processes that emerged
underlined this, and it was, in our view a strength of the work.
However, the ambiguity and uncertainty that it also produced was
too much for some people who wanted, quite naturally, a much
clearer definition and description of what they were being asked to
accept and, who, when this greater clarity was not forthcoming,
tended to opt out of further involvement. The problem of
transferring an attractive philosophy into a practical working
method was also a barrier which some people found too difficult to
overcome. It was not surprising that one of the Review Group
recommendations was that it was time for some definition of
participative management to be published.

Lastly, among the two thrids of the staff who were less interested there
was a certain level of apathy and lethargy which had been
commented on during the diagnosis, and we also experienced in our
dealings with some of the staff. One quotation from the Review
Group report says it all:

> "I am not sufficiently interested in my job to think about the
> organisation of Computer Division or its power
> structure."

These reactions were common throughout the division and help to explain the
attitudes of the staff who were broadly neutral to the project. Why the apparent
desire for participation was so much weaker in the lower grades is probably due
in some measure to the nature of the work. Two particular blocks of staff in this
region are in the data preparation and computer operating areas - basically
production oriented work, dominated by the technology, where the individual
has little direct control over the use of his or her time. The demands of the
machine dominate the task so that under the existing regime the individual has
hardly any time to allocate as he or she would wish, a prerequisite for the kind
of direct participation which requires discussion, debate and feedback.
Participation in these areas is therefore much more difficult than in areas where
technology is less intrusive and where people already have a degree of control
over their time. This means that there is a much greater onus on middle and
senior management in these technology dominated areas to encourage the
development and maintenance of participation and to provide the time for it.

Other conditions leading to this poor response were probably;

Lack of familiarity by the staff with the processes of group and committee working and the disciplines that these entail.

Poor facilities eg desks, separate quiet rooms, stationery, and access to typing and duplicating facilities etc.

The fact that participative management had had a later start, particularly in Data Preparation, than elsewhere.

A 'dependency orientation' to work and lower expectations about working life in general. This is probably the key feature and we discuss it further below.

As we mentioned above the question of the desire for participation in young ADP staff, and our assumption that it was a growing demand in today's society, were key themes in our diagnosis and in our broad philosophy. On the evidence from this project it would appear that we had not over estimated the extent of the desire, but we had been too sanguine about its infectious qualities.

Apathy towards participation and involvement is not an uncommon phenomenon. Foy and Gadon [6] report that "outsiders, especially British managers, point out that Swedish workers waste an astonishing amount of time in committee meetings, always at company expense. The Swedes retort that this is an essential part of developing involvement and worry instead that workers are too apathetic about participation." Given this concern about apathy, a later statement attributed to those same Swedish managers that participation is "a social imperative" may seem strange. Are they saying that people are demanding participation yet don't want it when they get it? It in fact highlights the difference between developing social values and individual behaviour.

The key to this apparent contradiction between social demands and individual apathy lies in our history. We have argued that the way work has been organised in the past, particularly in respect of relationships between management and staff is becoming increasingly unacceptable. Influenced by liberal trends in society ideas are being generated which suggest the desirability of more participation by employees in the work situation. These ideas are seen to be 'of the time' and the social value system is such that they seem to be 'right', to a growing consensus of people in society.

Ideas are an intellectual concept. They can be assimilated and accepted fairly quickly. Behavioural change generally requires a much longer time. Because of this those committed to, and trying to introduce, participation experience extreme frustration. The individual employee, especially at lower levels in the organisation, begins with possibly years of experience of traditional us/them

116

attitudes, where he has been dependent upon and felt manipulated by employers. Manipulation has created mistrust. Specialisation has conditioned workers to expect to contribute nothing but their specialism.

Those higher in the organisational hierarchy also experience difficulties in behavioural adaption. They have often made significant sacrifices earlier in their careers to achieve their existing position. In their role of 'bureaucratic man' they enjoy benefits of higher rewards, security, privacy and status. They are anxious to maintain the benefits they have accumulated. Paradoxically as 'social man' they may be among the foremost advocates of "intellectual level" participation!

Again nearer home, the Note of Dissent by Nicholas Wilson, in tbe Bullock Report [5] refers to "the relative apathy" on the part of employees to the concepts of industrial democracy; and even in such a shining example of democracy at work as the Scott Bader Commonwealth there is concern that "not enough members were interested in the principles behind the community" (Guardian, Monday 7 March 1976).

Yet despite all this concern about apathy and disinterested attitudes there seems to be a growing consensus that work place democracy and participation is here to stay. Foy and Gadon [6] conclude from their study of participation in three countries (United States, United Kingdom, Sweden) that there exists a "growing push from the workforce for greater involvement in decisions and more satisfaction at work" and that "the trend is an international one".

On reflection the strength of the commitment to participation in Computer Division during a relatively short experience did not diminish in strength and produced some remarkable changes. In summary then, our conclusion about this overall desire for participation is that our original diagnosis and earlier intuitive estimate of about a third of the whole staff who were interested and involved was borne out in practice; that of the more qualified staff ie the broad management grades, perhaps a half felt this way; that we did not succeed in spreading the desire very much further among the uncommitted and that for a variety of reasons to do with the nature of the work and individual expectations and understanding a significant proportion of staff were unaffected or uncommitted to the philosophy of participation. Whilst it is dangerous to generalise from one particular case, we see no fundamental reason to doubt that broadly similar conclusions might be drawn about employing organisations as a whole. If this were the case, the prospect of obtaining the kind of commitment, involvement and release of energy from between a third to a half of the public sector that we experienced in Computer Division in such a short time is an exciting one.

Summing up the problem of apathy and the desire for participation one can suggest that the whole existing work ethic is increasingly out of tune with social values. Yet the legacy of that work ethic, dependency, hostility and vested interests, inhibits positive initiatives to meet social needs. There are two likely ways things can go, one is a change in degree, the other is a change in the order of things.

A change in the order of things will involve organisational revolution - work-ins, and the formation of co-operatives are possible models.

A change in degree is an adaptive process - the creation of a 'new bureaucracy'.

Our evidence is that the latter is a viable strategy which can meet the social need.

We end with a particularly apposite piece of philosophical prediction from well before the age of the electronic computer. In 1928, Aldous Huxley wrote in "Point, Counterpoint":

> "Mechanical progress means more specialisation and standardisation of work ... means diminution of initiative and creativeness, means more intellectualism and thus progressive atrophy of all the vital and fundamental things in human nature and means increased boredom and restlessness, means finally a kind of individual madness that can only result in social revolution."

So many of the trends that we can observe in the society of the 1970s were foreseen by Huxley that we feel his warning, if warning it is, should be taken very seriously. Our observations suggest that the remedy to this "individual madness" is within our grasp. It lies, fundamentally, in a recognition by all concerned - managers, union officials and each member of staff that each individual has gifts which need to be developed and expressed through his or her work, and that the sum of these unique contributions can be a vital, effective and exciting working community. Such concepts are not Utopian, nor do they turn a blind eye to the realities of conflict and the plurality of interests; rather they advocate a new understanding of the status of the individual in organisations and the processes by which the potential which lies in us all can be more fully liberated.

NOTES

[1] Schein E.H., Organisational Psychology, Prentice Hall, 1965

[2] Report of the Committee of Inquiry on Industrial Democracy, Chairman, Lord Bullock, Cmnd 6706, HMSO January 1977

[3] Davies, H. "The Creighton Report" Hamish Hamilton 1976

[4] Sofer, C. "Organisations in Theory and Practice" Heinemann, 1972

[5]   Miner, J.B., "The Real Crunch in Managerial Manpower" Harvard Business Review Vol. 51, No6, Nov-Dec, 1973.

[6]   Foy, N. and Gadon, H. "Worker participation: contrasts in three countries" Harvard Business Review, Vol. 55, No3, May-June, 1976.